Standardized Test Skill Builders for Math

Grades 3–4

New York • Toronto • London • Auckland • Sydney
Mexico City • New Delhi • Hong Kong

Cover design by Jaime Lucero and Kelli Thompson
Interior design by Creative Pages, Inc.
Interior illustrations by Kate Flanagan

ISBN 0-439-16232-7

Contents

Introduction to Teachers

We all know how important it is for students to do well on tests. This book is one in a series designed to help you help your students become better test takers.

In the past few years, many statewide tests and national standardized tests have undergone significant changes, not just in *what* they measure but also in *how* they measure content and skills. The examples and practice tests in this book reflect the latest developments in testing and are designed to look like the state and national tests. Features include:

- An emphasis on thinking and problem-solving strategies
- A variety of question types, including multiple-choice items, open-ended questions, and problems with more than one correct approach
- Problems that involve real-world applications

This book covers all of the significant math skills tested on the five most widely used standardized tests: the *CTBS TerraNova, Metropolitan Achievement Test, Stanford Achievement Test, Iowa Test of Basic Skills,* and *California Achievement Test*. It also uses the same kinds of questions and the same formats as the standardized tests.

Practice Activities

There are seven Practice sections in this book, followed by a full-length Math Test. Each Practice focuses on specific math strategies and skills. Features of each Practice include:

- Sample items for students to work through
- Hints on how to answer each type of question
- Explanations of the correct answers
- Reminders to help students during an actual test
- A Practice Test to help students apply what they have learned

Procedures

We recommend that you first teach the targeted math skills before you use this book. Then work through each Practice with your students. Using the overhead with transparencies of assigned pages helps students understand the process of carefully reading the problems and working through solutions. Discuss the sample questions and how to get the right answers, and then have students take the Practice Test. Use the Answer Keys at the back of the book to score each test, or have students score the tests themselves and record their scores in the box at the end of each Practice Test. Either way, make sure students have ample opportunity to study their own tests and learn from any mistakes they might have made. When students have completed all the practice activities, administer the Math Test (beginning on page 35). The Math Test has a total of 70 items, including several open-ended tasks. It will take about one and a half hours to complete.

Students who complete the activities in this book will become familiar with the kinds of questions and problems they will see on "real" tests, and they will have a new arsenal of techniques and strategies for getting better test scores.

Problem-Solving Strategies

PRACTICE 1: SAMPLE

HINT: Read each problem carefully.

Directions
Choose the best answer to each question.

A **Tickets to the school play cost $6 each. Which number sentence should be used to find how much 3 tickets will cost?**

Ⓐ $6 + 3 = □
Ⓑ $6 − 3 = □
Ⓒ $6 × 3 = □
Ⓓ $6 ÷ 3 = □

B **A total of 204 students go to Park Elementary School. On Monday, 37 students were absent. Which numbers give the best estimate of how many students were in school on Monday?**

Ⓕ 200 − 30
Ⓖ 200 − 40
Ⓗ 210 − 30
Ⓙ 210 − 40

HINT: Look for key words to solve each problem.

C **Cynthia went for a hike with her family. She hiked an average of 2 miles every hour. What else do you need to know to find out how many miles Cynthia hiked in all?**

Ⓐ how many people in her family
Ⓑ how many hours she hiked
Ⓒ how fast she hiked the first mile
Ⓓ how much she weighs

Finding the Answers to Practice 1: Sample

To answer question **A**, you need to decide whether you should add, subtract, multiply, or divide. Since one ticket costs $6, you could add $6 + $6 + $6 to figure out how much 3 tickets will cost. But $6 + $6 + $6 is not one of the answers given. Instead, you could multiply the cost of one ticket ($6) by the number of tickets you want to buy (3) to find the total cost. Answer **C**, $6 × 3 = □, is correct.

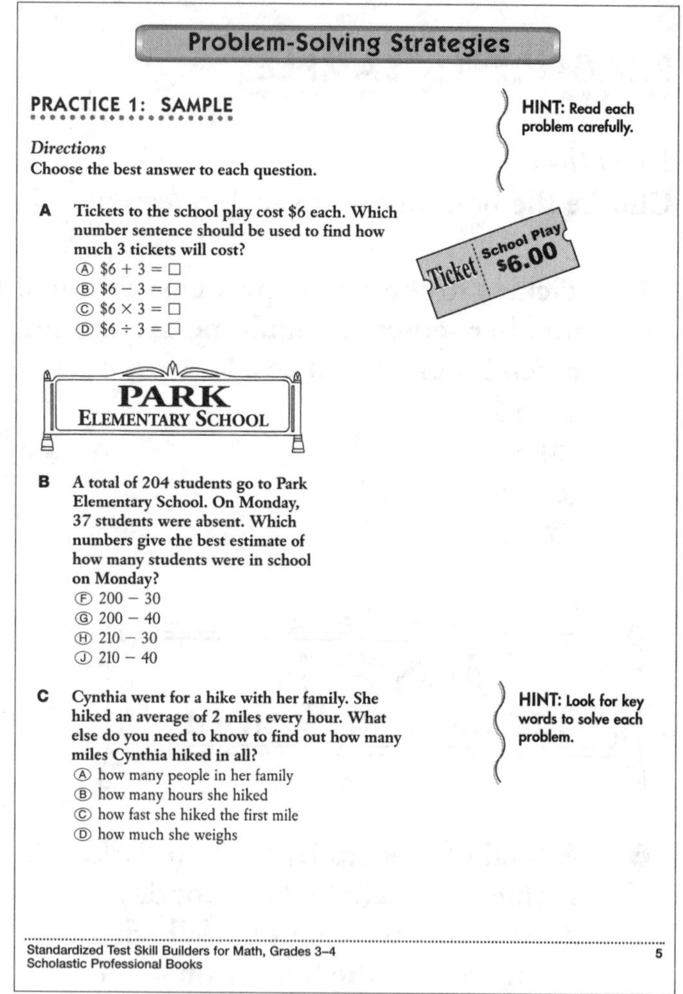

Problem-Solving Strategies

PRACTICE 1: SAMPLE

HINT: Read each problem carefully.

Directions
Choose the best answer to each question.

A Tickets to the school play cost $6 each. Which number sentence should be used to find how much 3 tickets will cost?
Ⓐ $6 + 3 = □
Ⓑ $6 − 3 = □
Ⓒ $6 × 3 = □
Ⓓ $6 ÷ 3 = □

B A total of 204 students go to Park Elementary School. On Monday, 37 students were absent. Which numbers give the best estimate of how many students were in school on Monday?
Ⓕ 200 − 30
Ⓖ 200 − 40
Ⓗ 210 − 30
Ⓙ 210 − 40

C Cynthia went for a hike with her family. She hiked an average of 2 miles every hour. What else do you need to know to find out how many miles Cynthia hiked in all?
Ⓐ how many people in her family
Ⓑ how many hours she hiked
Ⓒ how fast she hiked the first mile
Ⓓ how much she weighs

HINT: Look for key words to solve each problem.

Standardized Test Skill Builders for Math, Grades 3–4
Scholastic Professional Books 5

Question **B** involves estimating. To find the best estimate of how many students went to school on Monday, you need to round each number to the nearest ten. So if you round 204 to 200 and round 37 to 40, then the best estimate is 200 − 40. Answer **G** is correct.

To answer question **C**, you need to decide what information you will need to figure out how many miles Cynthia hiked in all. First, you can eliminate any answers that you know are wrong. Knowing how many people there are in Cynthia's family (answer **A**) will not help, and knowing how much Cynthia weighs (answer **D**) will not help. That leaves two possible answers. The problem says Cynthia hiked an average of 2 miles every hour, so you really don't need to know how fast she hiked the first mile (answer **C**). To find how many miles she hiked, you will need to know how many hours she hiked. Answer **B** is correct.

REMINDERS: As you take the Practice Test, remember these hints.

✔ Read each problem carefully to make sure you know what it is asking for.

✔ Look for key words and numbers to help you solve the problem.

✔ In question A, for example, the key words and numbers are *$6 each, 3 tickets, how much.*

✔ Eliminate any answers that you know are wrong.

✔ To estimate, round each number to the nearest 10 or 100.

✔ Check your answer to be sure it makes sense.

Problem-Solving Strategies

PRACTICE 1: TEST

Directions

Choose the best answer to each question.

Nell's Toy Cars

1 **Which number sentence should you use to find the total number of cars?**

Ⓐ $4 + 5 = \square$

Ⓑ $5 - 4 = \square$

Ⓒ $4 \times 5 = \square$

Ⓓ $5 \div 4 = \square$

2 **Josh has kept a record of the number of pages he read in one month. Which is the best estimate of the total number of pages he read?**

Ⓕ 500

Ⓖ 600

Ⓗ 700

Ⓙ 800

Number of Pages	
Week 1	98
Week 2	203
Week 3	197
Week 4	104

3 **Coach Bates got 28 shirts for the girls' soccer team. There are 19 girls on the team. How many extra shirts did she get?**

Ⓐ 47

Ⓑ 19

Ⓒ 10

Ⓓ 9

4 **Which of these is an incorrect number sentence to find the total number of baseballs?**

Ⓕ $6 \times 6 \times 6 =$

Ⓖ $6 + 6 + 6 =$

Ⓗ $6 \times 3 =$

Ⓙ $3 + 3 + 3 + 3 + 3 + 3 =$

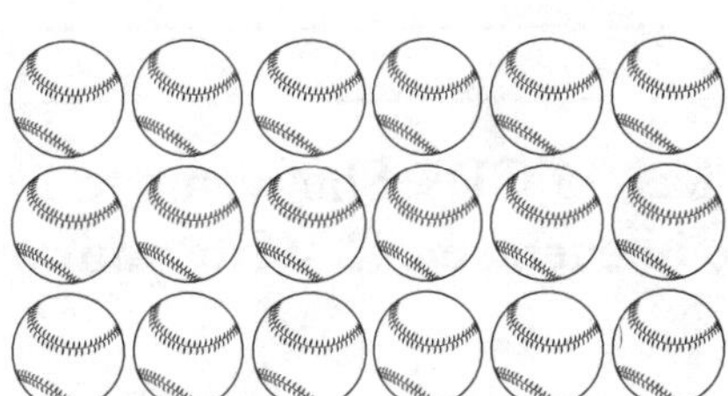

5 **Manuel has a large bag of marbles. He gives Elise 12 marbles from the bag. What else do you need to know to find out how many marbles Manuel has left?**

Ⓐ how many marbles fit in one bag

Ⓑ how many bags of marbles Elise has

Ⓒ what kinds of marbles they are

Ⓓ how many marbles Manuel had in the bag to start with

6 There are 78 girls and 91 boys at a summer camp. Which numbers give the best estimate of the total number of children at the camp?

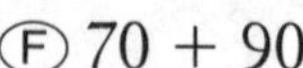

Ⓕ 70 + 90
Ⓖ 70 + 100
Ⓗ 80 + 90
Ⓙ 80 + 100

7 The Calders are taking a trip to the Grand Canyon. They plan to travel about 290 miles each day. About how far will they travel in 3 days?

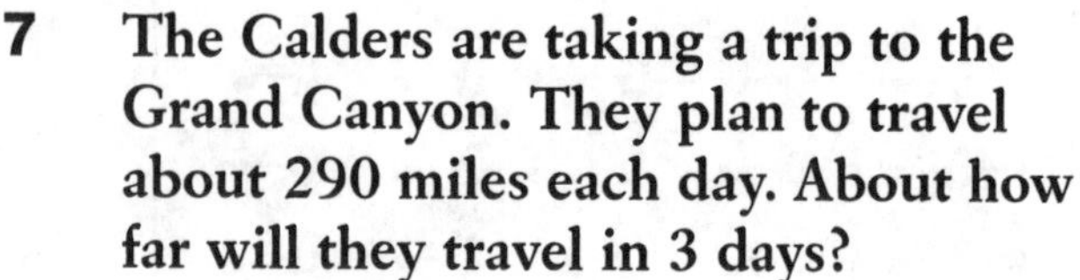

Ⓐ 900 miles
Ⓑ 800 miles
Ⓒ 600 miles
Ⓓ 300 miles

8 Kim loves to swim. She goes to the pool 5 days a week to swim laps. What else do you need to know to find out how many laps Kim swam last week?

Ⓕ how many laps she swam each day
Ⓖ which days of the week she swam
Ⓗ how many laps she can swim in one hour
Ⓙ how long it takes her to swim one lap

9 Lenny has 450 stamps in his stamp collection. At a stamp show, he sells 52 of his stamps. Then he buys 85 new stamps. How many stamps does he have in his collection now? Write your answer below. Show your work.

____

____

10 Tasha has 96 CDs. She wants to group them into 8 equal stacks. How many CDs will be in each stack? Write your answer below. Show your work.

____

____

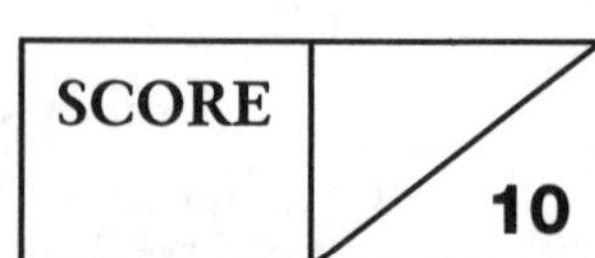

Using Whole Numbers

PRACTICE 2: SAMPLE

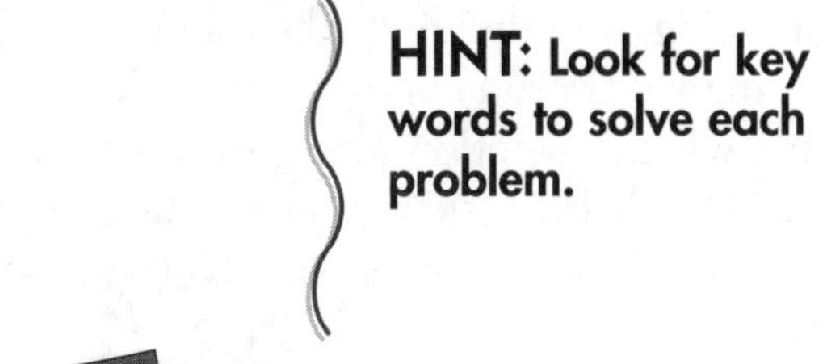

HINT: Look for key words to solve each problem.

Directions
Solve each problem.

A Ronnie sent 11 e-mail messages on Saturday and 18 messages on Sunday. How many messages did she send in all?

Ⓐ 7
Ⓑ 19
Ⓒ 27
Ⓓ 29

HINT: Write a number sentence to solve each problem.

B Tanya had 35 books. She gave 7 books to a friend. How many did she have left?

Ⓕ 42
Ⓖ 38
Ⓗ 32
Ⓙ 28

C Troy has 15 fruit roll-ups. He wants to share them with his friends. He splits the roll-ups into 3 equal groups. How many roll-ups are in each group?

Ⓐ 12
Ⓑ 5
Ⓒ 4
Ⓓ 3
Ⓔ None of these

D

$$\begin{array}{r} 47 \\ +\ 14 \\ \hline \end{array}$$

Ⓕ 62
Ⓖ 53
Ⓗ 51
Ⓙ 33
Ⓚ None of these

Finding the Answers to Practice 2: Sample

These problems involve adding, subtracting, multiplying, and dividing whole numbers. To solve the word problem in question **A**, you must decide which operation to use. Ronnie sent 11 messages *and* 18 messages, so you must add the numbers to find *how many in all:* $11 + 18 = 29$. Answer **D** is correct.

In question **B**, the key words "gave" and "how many left" tell you that you must subtract to find the correct answer. You know that Tanya had 35 books, and she gave 7 away: $35 - 7 = 28$. Answer **J** is correct.

In question **C**, Troy wants to split 15 fruit roll-ups equally in 3 groups, so you need to divide: $15 \div 3 = 5$. Answer **B** is correct.

Notice that in questions **C** and **D**, the last answer choice is "None of these." If you cannot find the correct answer, mark "None of these."

To answer question **D**, compute: $47 + 14 = 61$. The sum is 61, but 61 is not one of the answer choices, so answer **K**, "None of these," is correct.

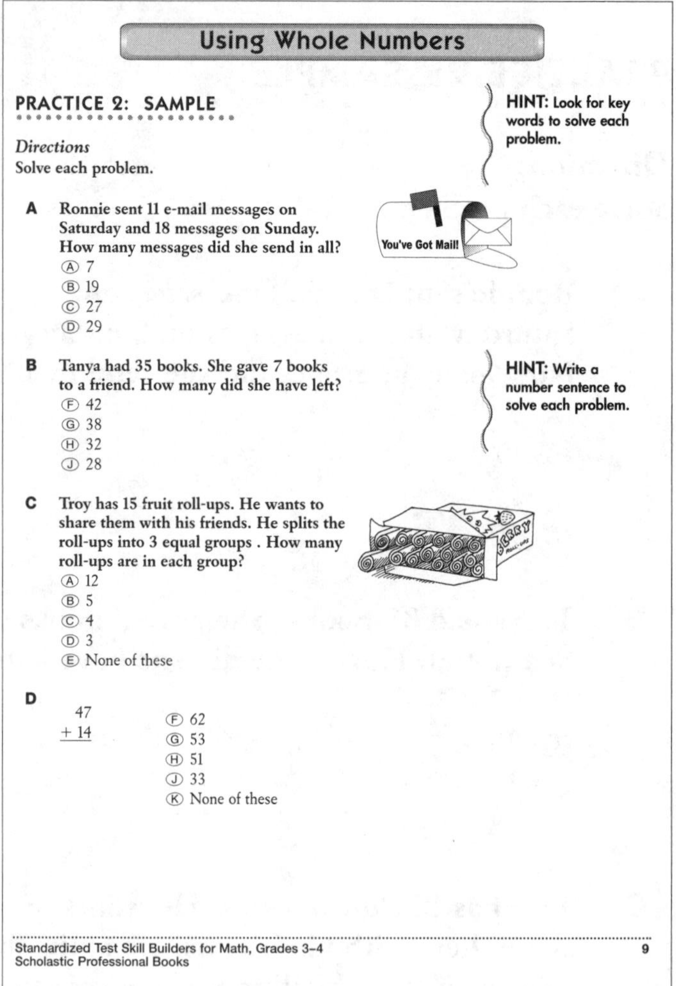

Using Whole Numbers

PRACTICE 2: SAMPLE

Directions
Solve each problem.

HINT: Look for key words to solve each problem.

A Ronnie sent 11 e-mail messages on Saturday and 18 messages on Sunday. How many messages did she send in all?
Ⓐ 7
Ⓑ 19
Ⓒ 27
Ⓓ 29

B Tanya had 35 books. She gave 7 books to a friend. How many did she have left?
Ⓕ 42
Ⓖ 38
Ⓗ 32
Ⓙ 28

HINT: Write a number sentence to solve each problem.

C Troy has 15 fruit roll-ups. He wants to share them with his friends. He splits the roll-ups into 3 equal groups . How many roll-ups are in each group?
Ⓐ 12
Ⓑ 5
Ⓒ 4
Ⓓ 3
Ⓔ None of these

D

$$\begin{array}{r} 47 \\ +\ 14 \\ \hline \end{array}$$

Ⓕ 62
Ⓖ 53
Ⓗ 51
Ⓙ 33
Ⓚ None of these

Standardized Test Skill Builders for Math, Grades 3–4
Scholastic Professional Books 9

REMINDERS: As you take the Practice Test, remember these hints.

✔ Read the problem carefully.

✔ Look for key words to help you decide whether you should add, subtract, multiply, or divide. For example, in question A, to find "how many in all," you need to add. In question C, to "split into equal groups," you need to divide.

✔ Write a number sentence to help you solve each problem.
The number sentence for question A is $11 + 18 = \square$.
The number sentence for question B is $35 - 7 = \square$.

✔ Check your answer carefully. If your answer is not given, mark "None of these."

Using Whole Numbers

PRACTICE 2: TEST

Directions

The Twinfield Elementary School soccer teams are having a bottle drive to help raise money for new uniforms. Answer numbers 1–6.

1 **Twinfield Elementary School has 4 soccer teams. Each team has 16 players. If each player gets a new uniform, how many uniforms will be needed?**

Ⓐ 4
Ⓑ 20
Ⓒ 32
Ⓓ 64

2 **The third-grade soccer team collected 594 cans and 321 bottles. What is the total number of cans and bottles collected?**

Ⓕ 915
Ⓖ 913
Ⓗ 815
Ⓙ 273

3 **Carla and Luiz collected 35 cans each. Amy collected 43 cans. How many cans did they collect all together?**

Ⓐ 73
Ⓑ 78
Ⓒ 103
Ⓓ 113
Ⓔ None of these

4 **A total of 32 students play on the third- and fourth-grade teams. On the day of the bottle drive, 8 players did not show up. How many players took part in the bottle drive?**

Ⓕ 4
Ⓖ 15
Ⓗ 24
Ⓙ 40
Ⓚ None of these

5 **The coach sent 8 players to collect bottles on Pine Street. The players split into 2 equal groups. How many players were in each group?**

Ⓐ 4
Ⓑ 6
Ⓒ 16
Ⓓ None of these

6 **Dustin collected 48 bottles, but 6 of them broke when he dropped them. How many bottles did he have left?**

Ⓕ 43
Ⓖ 44
Ⓗ 54
Ⓙ None of these

Directions

Ralph and his friends are visiting the zoo. Answer numbers 7–12.

7 **Last week 2367 people visited the zoo. This week 3041 people visited the zoo. What is the total number of people that visited the zoo for the two weeks?**

Ⓐ 674
Ⓑ 2671
Ⓒ 5398
Ⓓ 5408
Ⓔ None of these

8 **There are 726 animals in the zoo. Of all the animals, 193 are birds. How many of the animals are not birds?**

Ⓕ 919
Ⓖ 839
Ⓗ 633
Ⓙ 513
Ⓚ None of these

9 **The zookeeper is feeding the seals. She has 2 pails of fish. There are 40 fish in each pail. How many fish are there in all?**

Ⓐ 20
Ⓑ 42
Ⓒ 80
Ⓓ 84
Ⓔ None of these

10 **Ralph, Maria, and Kim got a bag of peanuts. There were 96 peanuts in the bag. The 3 friends split the peanuts evenly. How many peanuts did each person get?**

Ⓕ 32
Ⓖ 48
Ⓗ 93
Ⓙ 288
Ⓚ None of these

11 **The zoo offers group tours of up to 15 people per group. On Monday, the zoo gave 5 group tours. What is the greatest possible number of people in 5 groups? On the lines below, write a number sentence to help you solve the problem. Then write your answer.**

____

____

12 **At the zoo, Ralph and his friends counted 13 parrots, 4 ostriches, and 8 penguins. How many birds did they count in all? Write a number sentence to solve the problem. Then write your answer.**

____

____

Directions

For numbers 13–20, compute the answer to each problem.

13

$$\begin{array}{r} 371 \\ +\ 238 \\ \hline \end{array}$$

Ⓐ 609
Ⓑ 599
Ⓒ 509
Ⓓ 13
Ⓔ None of these

14

$$\begin{array}{r} 95 \\ -\ 71 \\ \hline \end{array}$$

Ⓕ 24
Ⓖ 26
Ⓗ 164
Ⓙ 166
Ⓚ None of these

15

$$\begin{array}{r} 105 \\ \times\ 5 \\ \hline \end{array}$$

Ⓐ 705
Ⓑ 525
Ⓒ 110
Ⓓ 100
Ⓔ None of these

16

$8\overline{)49}$

Ⓕ 6
Ⓖ 6 R7
Ⓗ 7
Ⓙ 7 R1
Ⓚ None of these

17

$56 + 24 =$

Ⓐ 32
Ⓑ 58
Ⓒ 70
Ⓓ 80
Ⓔ None of these

18

$741 - 32 =$

Ⓕ 773
Ⓖ 719
Ⓗ 709
Ⓙ 699
Ⓚ None of these

19

$4 \times 23 =$

Ⓐ 92
Ⓑ 82
Ⓒ 27
Ⓓ 19
Ⓔ None of these

20

$373 \div 7 =$

Ⓕ 50 R3
Ⓖ 52 R1
Ⓗ 53
Ⓙ 53 R2
Ⓚ None of these

SCORE	/ 20

Using Fractions and Decimals

PRACTICE 3: SAMPLE

Directions
Solve each problem.

A Jane has to make a picture showing $\frac{3}{8}$. Which of these figures has $\frac{3}{8}$ shaded?

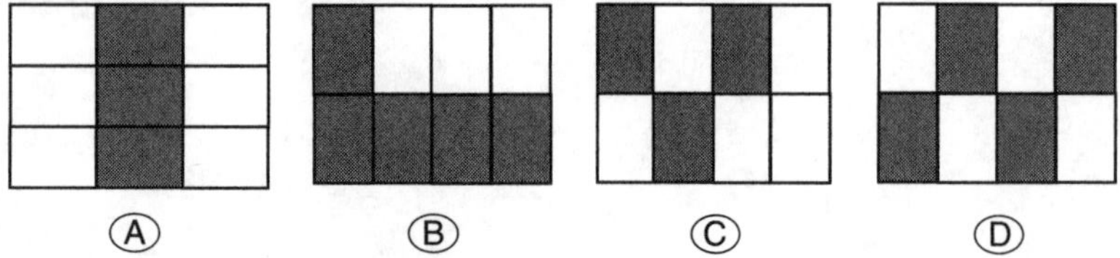

Ⓐ Ⓑ Ⓒ Ⓓ

B Sam was making berry muffins. He mixed together $\frac{1}{4}$ cup of blueberries and $\frac{1}{4}$ cup of cranberries in a bowl. How many cups of berries did he have in all?

Ⓕ $\frac{1}{4}$ cup
Ⓖ $\frac{1}{2}$ cup
Ⓗ $\frac{2}{8}$ cup
Ⓙ $\frac{3}{4}$ cup

HINT: Always rewrite fractions in their simplest form.

C This year, 7.5 inches of rain fell in Springfield. Last year, 5.2 inches of rain fell. How much more rain fell this year than last year?

Ⓐ 12.7 in.
Ⓑ 7.44 in.
Ⓒ 2.5 in.
Ⓓ 2.3 in.
Ⓔ None of these

HINT: To add or subtract decimals, be sure to line up the decimal points.

D Mrs. Liu had lunch at a sandwich shop. The Guest Check shows how much each item cost, but the waiter forgot to add the total. What was the total cost of Mrs. Liu's lunch? Write your answer.

____

Guest Check

Tuna Sandwich	$2.95
Fries	.75
Milk	.50
Cookie	.75
Total	?

Finding the Answers to Practice 3: Sample

These problems involve fractions and decimals. To find the answer to question **A**, you must find the figure that has a total of 8 parts with 3 of them shaded. Answer A cannot be correct because the figure has 9 parts. Each of the figures in answers B, C, and D has 8 parts. The only one that has 3 of the 8 parts shaded is answer **C**, which is correct.

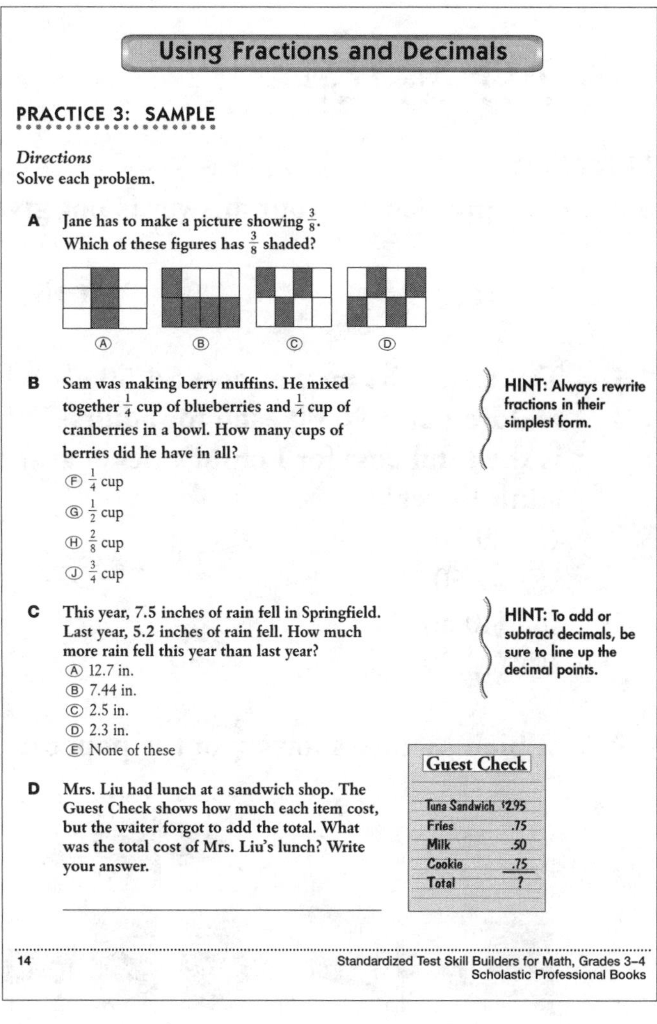

Using Fractions and Decimals

PRACTICE 3: SAMPLE

Directions
Solve each problem.

A Jane has to make a picture showing $\frac{3}{8}$. Which of these figures has $\frac{3}{8}$ shaded?

Ⓐ Ⓑ Ⓒ Ⓓ

B Sam was making berry muffins. He mixed together $\frac{1}{4}$ cup of blueberries and $\frac{1}{4}$ cup of cranberries in a bowl. How many cups of berries did he have in all?

Ⓕ $\frac{1}{4}$ cup
Ⓖ $\frac{1}{2}$ cup
Ⓗ $\frac{2}{8}$ cup
Ⓙ $\frac{3}{4}$ cup

HINT: Always rewrite fractions in their simplest form.

C This year, 7.5 inches of rain fell in Springfield. Last year, 5.2 inches of rain fell. How much more rain fell this year than last year?

Ⓐ 12.7 in.
Ⓑ 7.44 in.
Ⓒ 2.5 in.
Ⓓ 2.3 in.
Ⓔ None of these

HINT: To add or subtract decimals, be sure to line up the decimal points.

D Mrs. Liu had lunch at a sandwich shop. The Guest Check shows how much each item cost, but the waiter forgot to add the total. What was the total cost of Mrs. Liu's lunch? Write your answer.

Guest Check	
Tuna Sandwich	$2.95
Fries	.75
Milk	.50
Cookie	.75
Total	?

14 Standardized Test Skill Builders for Math, Grades 3–4
Scholastic Professional Books

In question **B**, the key words "how many in all" tell you that you must add to find the correct answer: $\frac{1}{4}$ cup + $\frac{1}{4}$ cup = $\frac{2}{4}$ cup. Then you rewrite the fraction in its simplest form: $\frac{2}{4} = \frac{1}{2}$. The answer is $\frac{1}{2}$ cup. Answer **G** is correct.

To solve the problem in question **C**, you must decide whether to add or subtract. The key words "how much more" tell you that you have to subtract to find how much more rain fell this year. 7.5 in. − 5.2 in. = 2.3 in. Answer **D** is correct.

Notice that in question C, the last answer choice is "None of these." If you cannot find the correct answer, mark "None of these."

To find the total cost in question **D**, add the costs on the Guest Check. Be sure to line up the decimal points correctly. The answer is $4.95.

$$\begin{array}{r} \$2.95 \\ .75 \\ .50 \\ +\ .75 \\ \hline \$4.95 \end{array}$$

REMINDERS: As you take the Practice Test, remember these hints.

- ✔ Look for key words to help you decide whether you should add or subtract. For example, in question B, to find *how many in all* you need to add.
- ✔ Write a number sentence to help you solve each problem.
- ✔ The number sentence for question C is 7.5 in. − 5.2 in. = □.
- ✔ When adding or subtracting fractions with like denominators, add or subtract only the numerators.
- ✔ Always rewrite fractions in their simplest form.
- ✔ To add or subtract decimals, line up the decimal points.
- ✔ Check your answer carefully.

PRACTICE 3: TEST

Directions

Solve each problem. If your answer is not given, mark "None of these."

At the Movies

1 Tickets to the movies cost $4.50 each for children and $6.00 each for adults. What is the total cost for 1 child's ticket and 1 adult ticket?

Ⓐ $9.00
Ⓑ $9.50
Ⓒ $10.50
Ⓓ $12.00

2 Which picture shows $\frac{2}{3}$ of the popcorn boxes shaded?

3 Mike and Joe got a pizza after the movie. Mike ate $\frac{1}{8}$ of the pizza. Joe ate $\frac{3}{8}$. How much of the pizza did they eat?

Ⓐ $\frac{1}{4}$ Ⓒ $\frac{4}{16}$

Ⓑ $\frac{5}{8}$ Ⓓ $\frac{1}{2}$

4 Suzi paid $4.50 for a ticket to the movies. Then she bought popcorn for $1.25 and a soda for $1.05. How much did she spend in all?

Ⓕ $6.80
Ⓖ $6.70
Ⓗ $5.75
Ⓙ $5.55
Ⓚ None of these

5 Karen saw 2 movies on Saturday. The first movie lasted $1\frac{1}{4}$ hours. The second movie lasted $1\frac{3}{4}$ hours. How long did the 2 movies last in all?

Ⓐ $2\frac{1}{2}$ hours

Ⓑ 3 hours

Ⓒ $3\frac{1}{2}$ hours

Ⓓ $3\frac{3}{4}$ hours

Ⓔ None of these

6 Shem stood in line at the snack bar for 6.4 minutes. Lisa stood in line for 9.2 minutes. How much longer did Lisa stand in line?

Ⓕ 2.2 minutes

Ⓖ 3.2 minutes

Ⓗ 3.8 minutes

Ⓙ 15.6 minutes

Ⓚ None of these

7 Ian and Lauren were going to the movies. Ian and his mom drove 1.25 miles to Lauren's house. Then they drove 2.5 miles to the movie theater. How many miles did they travel in all? Write your answer.

____

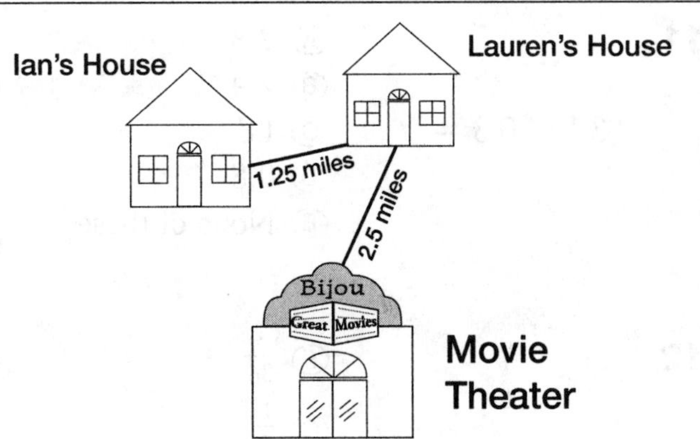

8 Jonas bought a huge candy bar. He ate $\frac{1}{5}$ of the bar during the movie. He gave $\frac{2}{5}$ of the bar to a friend. How much of the candy bar was left? Write your answer and draw a picture showing how much of the candy bar was left.

____

Directions

For numbers 9–16, compute.

9

$2.10 + 0.25 =$

Ⓐ 1.35
Ⓑ 2.12
Ⓒ 2.35
Ⓓ 4.60
Ⓔ None of these

10

$\frac{7}{9} - \frac{3}{9} =$

Ⓕ 4
Ⓖ $\frac{1}{3}$
Ⓗ $\frac{10}{9}$
Ⓙ $\frac{4}{9}$
Ⓚ None of these

11

$3.1 - 0.3 =$

Ⓐ 2.8
Ⓑ 2.4
Ⓒ 1.8
Ⓓ 0.8
Ⓔ None of these

12

$\frac{5}{6} + \frac{1}{6} =$

Ⓕ $\frac{5}{36}$
Ⓖ $\frac{1}{6}$
Ⓗ $\frac{1}{2}$
Ⓙ $1\frac{1}{6}$
Ⓚ None of these

13

$$\begin{array}{r} 6.42 \\ +\ 1.00 \\ \hline \end{array}$$

Ⓐ 74.2
Ⓑ 7.42
Ⓒ 7.042
Ⓓ 0.742
Ⓔ None of these

14

$7.34 - 3.99 =$

Ⓕ 0.335
Ⓖ 3.25
Ⓗ 3.35
Ⓙ 33.5
Ⓚ None of these

15

$$\begin{array}{r} 5\frac{3}{5} \\ +\ 2\frac{1}{5} \\ \hline \end{array}$$

Ⓐ $3\frac{2}{5}$
Ⓑ $3\frac{4}{5}$
Ⓒ $7\frac{2}{5}$
Ⓓ $7\frac{4}{5}$
Ⓔ None of these

16

$\frac{9}{10} - \frac{3}{10} =$

Ⓕ $\frac{12}{10}$
Ⓖ $\frac{3}{5}$
Ⓗ $\frac{2}{3}$
Ⓙ $\frac{1}{2}$
Ⓚ None of these

SCORE	/ 16

Number Concepts

PRACTICE 4: SAMPLE

> **HINT:** Look for key words in each question.

Directions
Choose the best answer to each question.

A **What is the value of the 3 in 4238?**
Ⓐ 3
Ⓑ 30
Ⓒ 300
Ⓓ 3000

B **Which is another way to write five thousands, two tens, and six ones?**
Ⓕ 5260
Ⓖ 5261
Ⓗ 5216
Ⓙ 5026

C **Use estimation to find the problem with the largest answer.**

Ⓐ	Ⓑ	Ⓒ	Ⓓ
686 + 98	521 + 177	541 + 142	563 + 195

> **HINT:** Try each answer choice to find the one that is correct.

D **Members of the Reading Club read a certain number of books each year. So far, Kit has read $\frac{3}{4}$ of the total, Joel has read $\frac{2}{3}$, Marta has read $\frac{1}{2}$, and Luz has read $\frac{1}{6}$. Who has read the most books?**
Ⓕ Kit
Ⓖ Joel
Ⓗ Marta
Ⓙ Luz

E **For a chili recipe, Mr. Nicholson used $\frac{6}{10}$ of a pound of beef. How is this amount written as a decimal?**
Ⓐ 0.006
Ⓑ 0.06
Ⓒ 0.6
Ⓓ 6.0

Finding the Answers to Practice 4: Sample

This practice involves number concepts, such as place value, rounding, and comparing and ordering whole numbers, fractions, and decimals. Question **A** is a question about place value. The number 4238 is made up of 4 *thousands,* 2 *hundreds,* 3 *tens,* and 8 *ones*. The value of the 3 in 4238 is 3 tens, or 30. Answer **B** is correct.

In question **B**, you must identify the numerals for a number expressed in words: 5000 + 20 + 6 = 5026. The correct answer is **J**.

When you don't need to know exactly how much or how many, you can estimate to find a number that is close to the exact number and tells about how much or *about* how many. In question **C**, rounding to the nearest hundred will help you quickly estimate the sum in each problem. Then you can compare the answers to determine which is the largest. The sums in answers B, C, and D are each about 700. The sum in answer A is about 800. **A** is correct.

To solve question **D**, you must compare the fractions to see which one is largest. To do this, you must rename the fractions with like denominators. All four fractions can be renamed with 12 as the denominator: $\frac{3}{4} = \frac{9}{12}$; $\frac{2}{3} = \frac{8}{12}$; $\frac{1}{2} = \frac{6}{12}$; $\frac{1}{6} = \frac{2}{12}$. By comparing these fractions, you can see that $\frac{3}{4}$ is greatest, so Kit has read the most books. Answer **F** is correct.

To solve question **E**, you must write the fraction $\frac{6}{10}$ as a decimal. You can change any fraction to a decimal by dividing the numerator by the denominator: 6 ÷ 10 = 0.6. Answer **C** is correct.

Number Concepts

PRACTICE 4: SAMPLE

Directions
Choose the best answer to each question.

HINT: Look for key words in each question.

A What is the value of the 3 in 4238?
Ⓐ 3
Ⓑ 30
Ⓒ 300
Ⓓ 3000

B Which is another way to write five thousands, two tens, and six ones?
Ⓕ 5260
Ⓖ 5261
Ⓗ 5216
Ⓙ 5026

C Use estimation to find the problem with the largest answer.

Ⓐ 686 + 98 Ⓑ 521 + 177 Ⓒ 541 + 142 Ⓓ 563 + 195

D Members of the Reading Club read a certain number of books each year. So far, Kit has read $\frac{3}{4}$ of the total, Joel has read $\frac{2}{3}$, Marta has read $\frac{1}{2}$, and Luz has read $\frac{1}{6}$. Who has read the most books?
Ⓕ Kit
Ⓖ Joel
Ⓗ Marta
Ⓙ Luz

HINT: Try each answer choice to find the one that is correct.

E For a chili recipe, Mr. Nicholson used $\frac{6}{10}$ of a pound of beef. How is this amount written as a decimal?
Ⓐ 0.006
Ⓑ 0.06
Ⓒ 0.6
Ⓓ 6.0

Standardized Test Skill Builders for Math, Grades 3–4 19
Scholastic Professional Books

REMINDERS: As you take the Practice Test, remember these hints.

✔ Look for key words in each question (such as *greater than, less than, most, least*).

✔ Try each answer choice to find the one that is correct.

✔ Estimate by rounding each number to the nearest 10, 100, or 1000.

✔ Check your answer to be sure it makes sense.

PRACTICE 4: TEST

Directions
Choose the best answer to each question.

Mia and her friends weighed themselves for a science project. Use the results shown below to answer numbers 1–3.

Pounds
Kate 63
Daren 72
Matt 68
Mia 66

1 Who weighs the most?
- Ⓐ Daren
- Ⓑ Matt
- Ⓒ Mia
- Ⓓ Kate

2 Which is the best estimate of how much Matt and Mia weigh together?
- Ⓕ 100 lb
- Ⓖ 120 lb
- Ⓗ 140 lb
- Ⓙ 160 lb

3 Which person's weight is an odd number?
- Ⓐ Kate
- Ⓑ Daren
- Ⓒ Matt
- Ⓓ Mia

4 What is the value of the 6 in 7625?
- Ⓕ 6 thousands
- Ⓖ 6 hundreds
- Ⓗ 6 tens
- Ⓙ 6 ones

5 Use estimation to find the problem with the largest answer.
- Ⓐ $547 - 98$
- Ⓒ $579 - 143$
- Ⓑ $498 - 59$
- Ⓓ $521 - 168$

6 Which number shows nine thousand three hundred seven?
- Ⓕ 937
- Ⓖ 9370
- Ⓗ 9037
- Ⓙ 9307

7 **A pot is $\frac{7}{10}$ filled with soup. How is this amount written as a decimal?**

Ⓐ 7.0
Ⓑ 0.7
Ⓒ 0.07
Ⓓ 0.007

8 **Which number should go in the box to make the number sentence true?**

$\square > 20.2$

Ⓕ 2.2
Ⓖ 20.2
Ⓗ 22.2
Ⓙ 2.02

9 **Mrs. Vasta is using four pieces of cloth to make a mural. The pieces measure $\frac{1}{6}$ yard, $\frac{2}{3}$ yard, $\frac{1}{2}$ yard, and $\frac{5}{12}$ yard. Which is smallest?**

Ⓐ $\frac{5}{12}$
Ⓑ $\frac{1}{2}$
Ⓒ $\frac{2}{3}$
Ⓓ $\frac{1}{6}$

10 **Third graders collected 531.19 pounds of trash for the recycling drive. What is this amount rounded to the nearest tenth?**

Ⓕ 532
Ⓖ 531.2
Ⓗ 531.19
Ⓙ 530

11 **Mr. Lopinski finished a road race in 3.092 hours. Which of these times is faster than Mr. Lopinski's?**

Ⓐ 4.0 hours
Ⓑ 3.90 hours
Ⓒ 3.20 hours
Ⓓ 3.08 hours

12 **The Murphy children compared how much they grew in a year. Which child's growth is <u>closest</u> to 2 inches?**

Ⓕ Ben: $1\frac{7}{8}$ in.
Ⓖ Lori: $1\frac{1}{4}$ in.
Ⓗ Trent: $2\frac{1}{3}$ in.
Ⓙ Eli: $2\frac{3}{4}$ in.

13 **A wedding ring contains 3.758 grams of gold. What is the value of the 5 in this number?**

Ⓐ 5 ones
Ⓑ 5 tens
Ⓒ 5 hundredths
Ⓓ 5 tenths

14 **The town of Waterbury has a population of 7254. What is this number rounded to the nearest hundred?**

Ⓕ 7200
Ⓖ 7250
Ⓗ 7300
Ⓙ 7400

SCORE	/ 14

PRACTICE 5: SAMPLE

Directions

The table shows how many adult and student helpers are needed for Davis School's Fall Fair. Use the table to answer each question.

Number of Helpers Needed		
Activity	**Adults**	**Students**
Face painting	12	6
Pumpkin carving	8	8
Three-legged race	4	1
Scavenger hunt	3	3
Bobbing for apples	6	2

A **For which fair activity are the most adult helpers needed?**

Ⓐ Face painting
Ⓑ Pumpkin carving
Ⓒ Scavenger hunt
Ⓓ Bobbing for apples

B **How many adult and student helpers are needed for the scavenger hunt?**

Ⓕ 5
Ⓖ 6
Ⓗ 8
Ⓙ 16

C **What is the average number of student helpers needed for each fair activity?**

Ⓐ 7
Ⓑ 5
Ⓒ 4
Ⓓ 2

HINT: Look back at the table to find the information you need.

Finding the Answers to Practice 5: Sample

To answer question **A**, compare the numbers in the "Adults" column. The greatest number, 12, goes with the face-painting activity, so **A** is the correct answer.

To answer question **B**, find the row of numbers for the scavenger hunt. Three adults and 3 students are needed for this activity; $3 + 3 = 6$, so answer **G** is correct.

Question **C** asks you to find the *average* number of students needed for each activity. To find the average, add together all the numbers of student helpers. Then divide this sum by the number of activities. $6 + 8 + 1 + 3 + 2 = 20$. $20 \div 5 = 4$. The average number of students needed for each activity is 4. Answer **C** is correct.

Interpreting Data

PRACTICE 5: SAMPLE

Directions
The table shows how many adult and student helpers are needed for Davis School's Fall Fair. Use the table to answer each question.

Number of Helpers Needed		
Activity	**Adults**	**Students**
Face painting	12	6
Pumpkin carving	8	8
Three-legged race	4	1
Scavenger hunt	3	3
Bobbing for apples	6	2

A **For which fair activity are the most adult helpers needed?**
Ⓐ Face painting
Ⓑ Pumpkin carving
Ⓒ Scavenger hunt
Ⓓ Bobbing for apples

B **How many adult and student helpers are needed for the scavenger hunt?**
Ⓕ 5
Ⓖ 6
Ⓗ 8
Ⓙ 16

C **What is the average number of student helpers needed for each fair activity?**
Ⓐ 7
Ⓑ 5
Ⓒ 4
Ⓓ 2

HINT: Look back at the table to find the information you need.

REMINDERS: As you take the Practice Test, remember these hints.

✔ Read each problem carefully.

✔ Look for key words in each question (such as *most, least, greater than, less than*).

✔ Look back at the table, graph, or chart to find the information you need for each question.

Interpreting Data

PRACTICE 5: TEST

Directions

The graph below shows the number of different types of animals at the Lake City Zoo. Use the graph to answer questions 1–3.

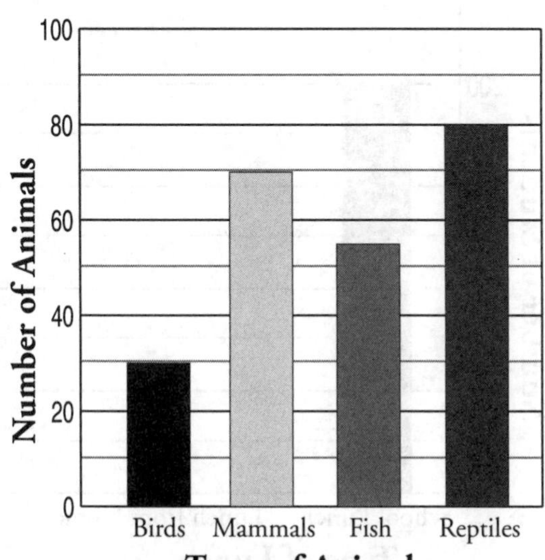

1 **The Lake City Zoo has the fewest of which type of animal?**

Ⓐ Birds　Ⓑ Mammals　Ⓒ Fish　Ⓓ Reptiles

2 **How many fish does the Lake City Zoo have?**

Ⓕ fewer than 40
Ⓖ between 40 and 50
Ⓗ between 50 and 60
Ⓙ more than 60

3 **About how many more reptiles than mammals are there at the Lake City Zoo?**

Ⓐ 40　Ⓑ 30　Ⓒ 20　Ⓓ 10

The table below shows clothing sizes according to height and weight. Use the table to answer questions 4–6.

Clothing Sizes		
Size	Height (*inches*)	Weight (*pounds*)
6	41–46	39–52
8	47–50	53–69
10	51–54	70–79
12	55–58	80–89
14	59–61	90–115

4 **Size 6 clothing is made for children who weigh how many pounds?**

Ⓕ 39–52　Ⓖ 41–46　Ⓗ 47–50　Ⓙ 53–69

5 **Lena is 52 inches tall and weighs 75 pounds. Which clothing size will fit her best?**

Ⓐ size 8　Ⓑ size 10　Ⓒ size 12　Ⓓ size 14

6 **Victor is 63 inches tall and weighs 110 pounds. A size 14 jacket will probably be**

Ⓕ too loose for him.
Ⓖ too short for him.
Ⓗ too tight for him.
Ⓙ too long for him.

The chart below shows how many pets were adopted from the animal shelter from January to April. Use the chart to answer questions 7–9.

Pets Adopted from Shelter				
Month	Cats	Kittens	Dogs	Puppies
Jan.	4	12	3	6
Feb.	5	8	5	7
Mar.	6	10	4	9
Apr.	2	9	6	10

7 In which month were the most pets adopted?

Ⓐ January　Ⓒ March
Ⓑ February　Ⓓ April

8 How many cats were adopted from January through April?

Ⓕ 17　Ⓗ 32
Ⓖ 18　Ⓙ 39

To answer questions 9 and 10, read the information below.

Mr. Chester bought a box of frozen juice pops to share with his class. The box of 30 pops contained 6 cherry, 6 grape, 9 lemon-lime, and 9 orange pops. Each student took a pop from the box without looking. Melvin was the first student to choose.

9 What chance did Melvin have of choosing a cherry pop?

Ⓐ $\frac{1}{30}$　Ⓒ $\frac{1}{6}$
Ⓑ $\frac{1}{24}$　Ⓓ $\frac{1}{5}$

10 What is the probability that Melvin got either a lemon-lime or orange pop?

Ⓕ $\frac{3}{10}$　Ⓗ $\frac{2}{3}$
Ⓖ $\frac{3}{5}$　Ⓙ $\frac{3}{4}$

To answer questions 11 and 12, read the information below.

At Morris School, the number of students who bring lunch from home is half the number of students who eat a school lunch. The graph below shows how many students eat school lunch.

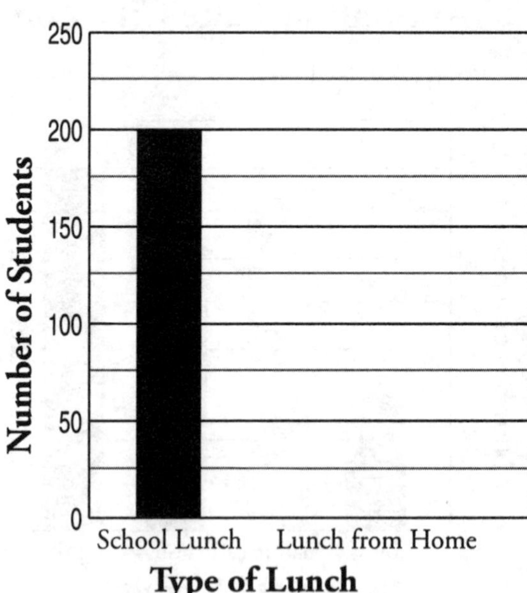

11 Finish the graph by drawing a bar that represents the number of students who bring lunch from home.

12 How many students bring a lunch from home?

____

SCORE	12

Measurement

PRACTICE 6: SAMPLE

> **HINT:** Read each problem carefully so you know what to look for.

Directions
Choose the best answer to each question.

A **Mrs. Butler wants to measure the volume of juice she squeezed from two oranges. Which unit should she use?**

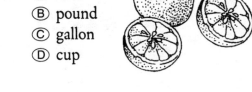

Ⓐ inch
Ⓑ pound
Ⓒ gallon
Ⓓ cup

B **Nick's sleeping bag is 2 meters long. What is the length of the sleeping bag in centimeters?**

Ⓕ 0.2 cm
Ⓖ 20 cm
Ⓗ 200 cm
Ⓙ 2000 cm

C **At 4:15, Lisa saw this note from her sister on the kitchen table.**

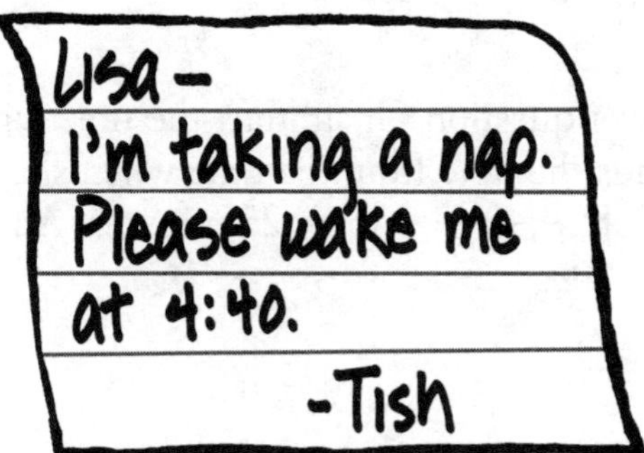

How much longer should Lisa let Tish sleep?

Ⓐ 15 minutes
Ⓑ 25 minutes
Ⓒ 40 minutes
Ⓓ 55 minutes

Finding the Answers to Practice 6: Sample

To answer question **A**, you must know what each unit is used to measure. Length is measured in inches, and weight is measured in pounds. Volume may be measured in cups or gallons. Since two oranges make only a small amount of juice, a cup is easier to use. The correct answer is **D**.

To answer question **B**, you have to change one unit of measure to another unit. Since 1 meter = 100 centimeters, then 2 m = 200 cm. Answer **H** is correct.

To answer question **C**, subtract the time when Lisa reads the note from the time when she should wake Tish: 4:40 − 4:15 = 25 minutes. Answer **B** is correct.

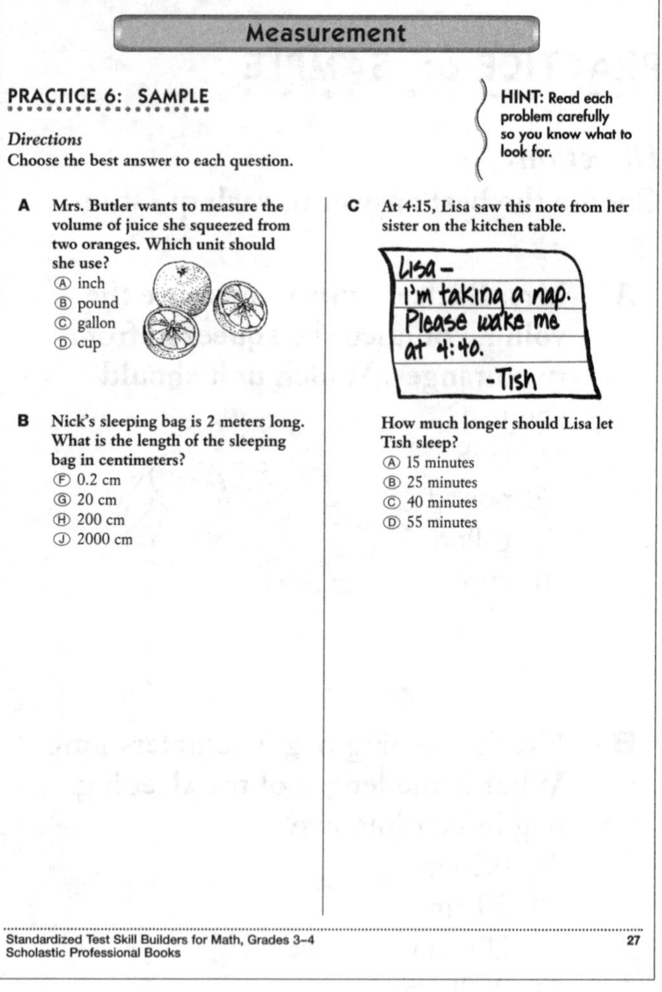

Measurement

PRACTICE 6: SAMPLE

Directions
Choose the best answer to each question.

HINT: Read each problem carefully so you know what to look for.

A Mrs. Butler wants to measure the volume of juice she squeezed from two oranges. Which unit should she use?
Ⓐ inch
Ⓑ pound
Ⓒ gallon
Ⓓ cup

B Nick's sleeping bag is 2 meters long. What is the length of the sleeping bag in centimeters?
Ⓕ 0.2 cm
Ⓖ 20 cm
Ⓗ 200 cm
Ⓙ 2000 cm

C At 4:15, Lisa saw this note from her sister on the kitchen table.

Lisa –
I'm taking a nap.
Please wake me
at 4:40.
-Tish

How much longer should Lisa let Tish sleep?
Ⓐ 15 minutes
Ⓑ 25 minutes
Ⓒ 40 minutes
Ⓓ 55 minutes

Standardized Test Skill Builders for Math, Grades 3–4
Scholastic Professional Books 27

REMINDERS: As you take the Practice Test, remember these hints.

✔ Read each problem carefully.

✔ Find key words that tell you what to look for. For example, in question B, the key words are *length in centimeters*.

✔ Write a number sentence to help you solve problems (like question C).

✔ Become familiar with both metric and standard measures.

Measurement

PRACTICE 6: TEST

Directions
Choose the best answer to each question.

1 Lara used 60 inches of string to make one braided bracelet. How many feet of string did she use?

Ⓐ 0.6 ft
Ⓑ 5 ft
Ⓒ 6 ft
Ⓓ 10 ft

2 A container of Jumbo Juice holds 1.2 liters. How many milliliters does the container hold?

Ⓕ 0.12 ml
Ⓖ 12 ml
Ⓗ 120 ml
Ⓙ 1200 ml

3 Which two clocks show the same time?

Ⓐ 3:02 

Ⓑ 7:40 

Ⓒ 12:15 

Ⓓ 2:00 

4 At 10:30, Andy put some bread in the oven to bake. The bread has to bake for 50 minutes. At what time will the bread be ready?

Ⓕ 10:50
Ⓖ 11:00
Ⓗ 11:20
Ⓙ 11:40

5 Sal found some change in her pocket. She had 9 quarters, 2 dimes, 1 nickel, and 4 pennies. How much money did Sal have?

Ⓐ $1.29
Ⓑ $1.54
Ⓒ $2.29
Ⓓ $2.54

6 Harry paid for his subway ride with 2 quarters, 4 nickels, and some dimes. If the subway ride cost $1.20, how many dimes did Harry pay?

Ⓕ 4 dimes
Ⓖ 5 dimes
Ⓗ 7 dimes
Ⓙ 8 dimes

7 The gym teacher wants to find out how far Tara can run in 10 seconds. Which unit should the gym teacher use?

Ⓐ inches
Ⓑ pints
Ⓒ yards
Ⓓ miles

8 **Chip filled a large bucket with sand and another with water. Which unit should he use to compare the mass of the buckets?**

Ⓕ grams
Ⓖ centimeters
Ⓗ milliliters
Ⓙ kilograms

9 **Tami is $4\frac{1}{2}$ feet tall. About how tall is the slide?**

Ⓐ 6 feet
Ⓑ 7 feet
Ⓒ 10 feet
Ⓓ 12 feet

10 **A crate holds 10 to 12 pounds of apples. How much would 6 crates of apples weigh?**

Ⓕ between 50 and 60 pounds
Ⓖ between 60 and 75 pounds
Ⓗ between 75 and 80 pounds
Ⓙ between 85 and 100 pounds

Use a centimeter ruler to answer questions 11 and 12.

11 **How tall is this stamp?**

Ⓐ 1 cm
Ⓑ 2 cm
Ⓒ 3 cm
Ⓓ 4 cm

12 **On Monday, Mrs. Stavros drove from River City to Johnston. On Tuesday, she drove from Johnston to Stillwater. How many kilometers did she drive in all? Write your answer.**

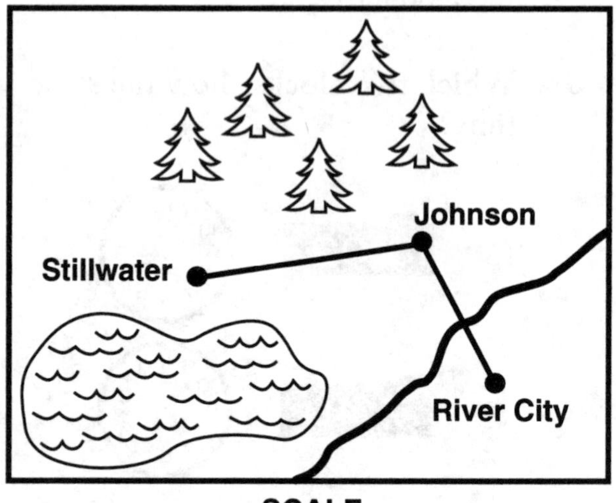

SCALE
1 centimeter = 10 kilometers

_______________ kilometers

SCORE	/12

Geometry

PRACTICE 7: SAMPLE

Directions
Choose the best answer to each question.

HINT: Read each problem carefully so you know what to look for.

A Jody wants to display her favorite stickers on a square sheet of paper. How many stickers can she fit on the square?

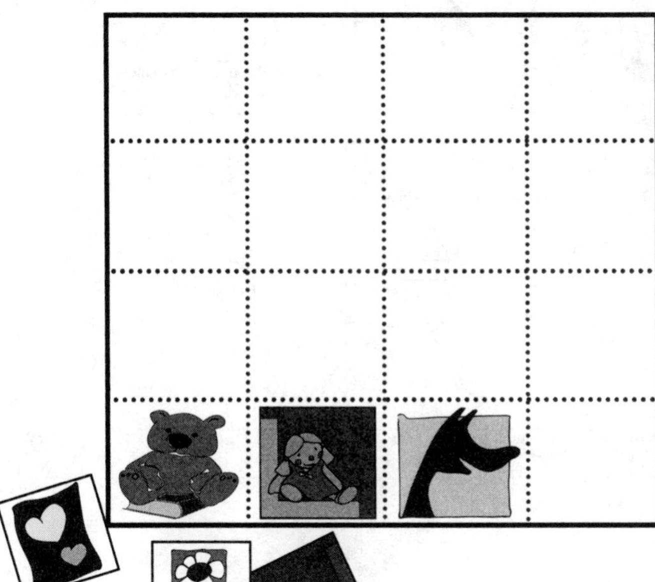

Ⓐ 9 Ⓒ 16
Ⓑ 12 Ⓓ 20

B Which figure has four equal sides?

Ⓕ  Ⓗ 

Ⓖ Ⓙ

C The dotted line shows where the figure was cut in half along a line of symmetry. What does the figure look like when the two halves are put together?

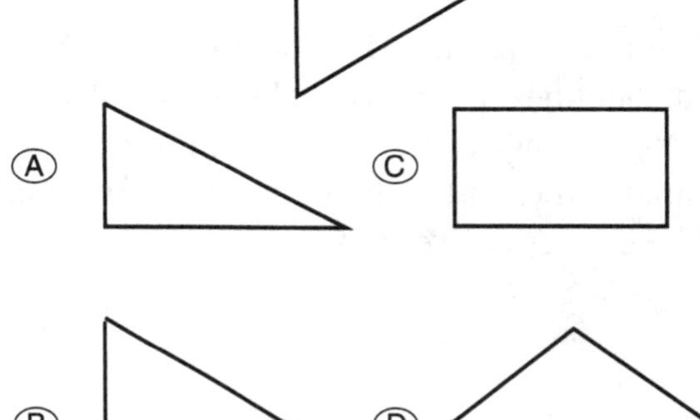

D Which lines are parallel?

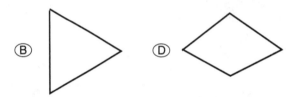

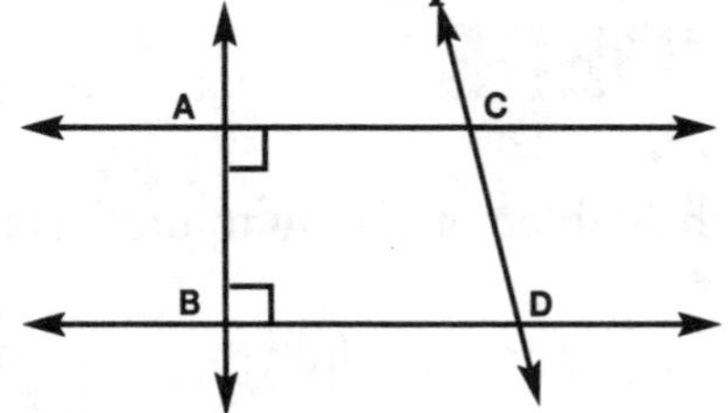

Ⓕ $\overleftrightarrow{AB}$ and $\overleftrightarrow{CD}$

Ⓖ $\overleftrightarrow{AB}$ and $\overleftrightarrow{AC}$

Ⓗ $\overleftrightarrow{CD}$ and $\overleftrightarrow{BD}$

Ⓙ $\overleftrightarrow{AC}$ and $\overleftrightarrow{BD}$

Finding the Answers to Practice 7: Sample

Question **A** is a question about area. Four rows of stickers with 4 stickers in each row will fit on the paper: $4 \times 4 = 16$. The correct answer is **C**.

To answer question **B**, you must understand the characteristics of different geometric figures. Of the figures shown, only the square has four equal sides. Answer **J** is correct.

Question **C** is a question about symmetry. A line of symmetry divides a figure into two halves that are mirror images of each other. When the figure shown is put together with its mirror image along the line of symmetry, the result is answer **B**.

To answer question **D**, you must find the parallel lines. Since parallel lines are always the same distance apart and do not intersect, the parallel lines in this figure must be $\overleftrightarrow{AC}$ and $\overleftrightarrow{BD}$. The correct answer is **J**.

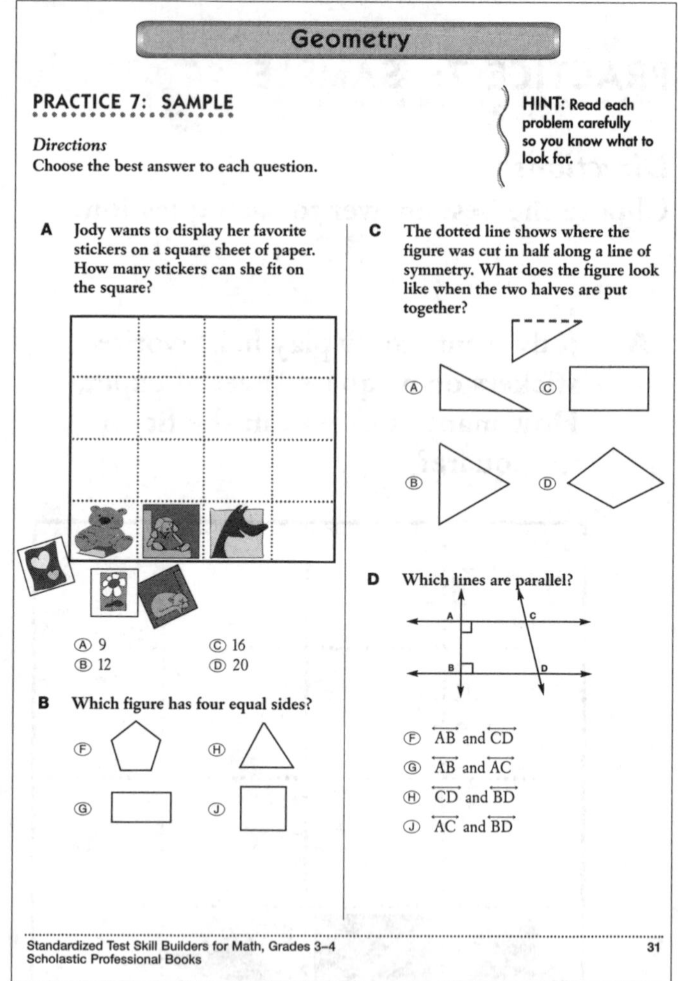

Geometry

PRACTICE 7: SAMPLE

HINT: Read each problem carefully so you know what to look for.

Directions
Choose the best answer to each question.

A Jody wants to display her favorite stickers on a square sheet of paper. How many stickers can she fit on the square?

Ⓐ 9
Ⓑ 12
Ⓒ 16
Ⓓ 20

B Which figure has four equal sides?

Ⓕ Ⓖ Ⓗ Ⓙ

C The dotted line shows where the figure was cut in half along a line of symmetry. What does the figure look like when the two halves are put together?

Ⓐ Ⓑ Ⓒ Ⓓ

D Which lines are parallel?

Ⓕ $\overleftrightarrow{AB}$ and $\overleftrightarrow{CD}$
Ⓖ $\overleftrightarrow{AB}$ and $\overleftrightarrow{AC}$
Ⓗ $\overleftrightarrow{CD}$ and $\overleftrightarrow{BD}$
Ⓙ $\overleftrightarrow{AC}$ and $\overleftrightarrow{BD}$

Standardized Test Skill Builders for Math, Grades 3–4
Scholastic Professional Books 31

REMINDERS: As you take the Practice Test, remember these hints.

✔ Read each problem carefully to understand what you are looking for.

✔ Look at the pictures carefully.

✔ Draw your own picture if it will help solve a problem.

PRACTICE 7: TEST

Directions
Choose the best answer to each question.

1 Which figure is a rectangle?

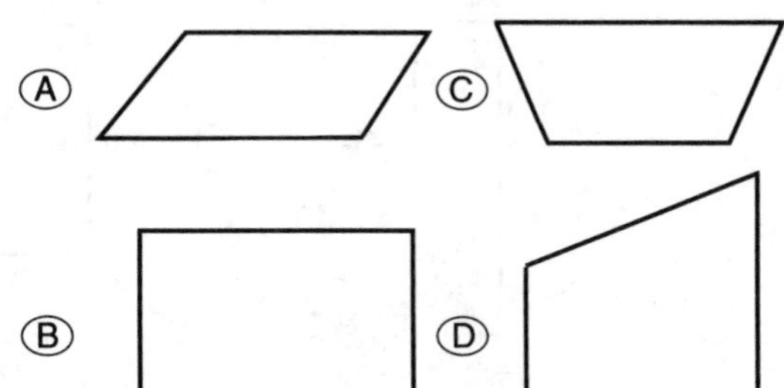

2 Which figure is a cube?

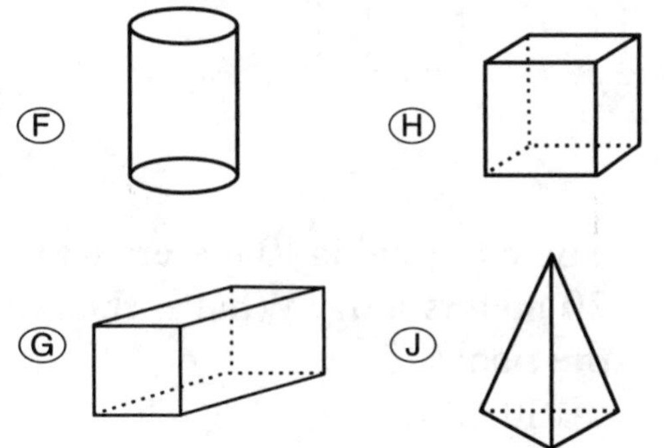

3 Which figure can be made by putting together the three figures below?

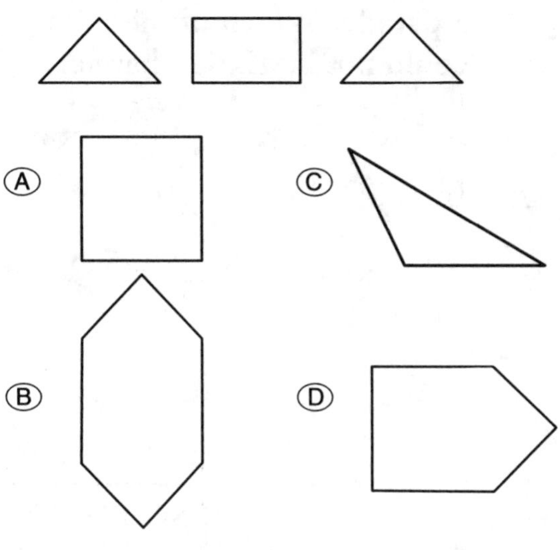

4 Which figure is congruent to Figure 1?

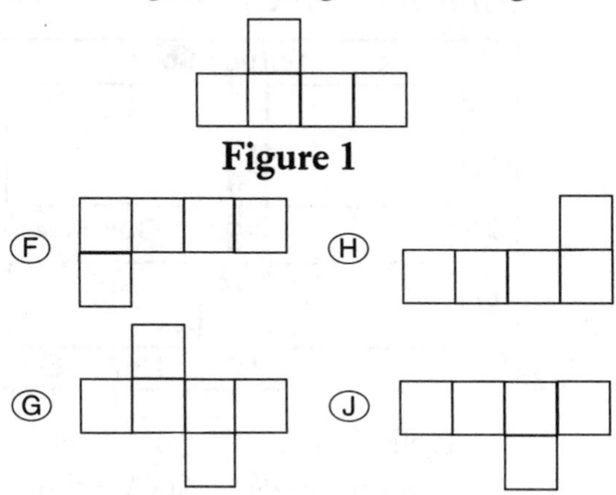

5 Gladys designed this greeting card. It is folded along a line of symmetry. How many trees can be seen in all when the card is unfolded?

Ⓐ 8 Ⓑ 6 Ⓒ 5 Ⓓ 3

6 Which of these figures is divided along a line of symmetry?

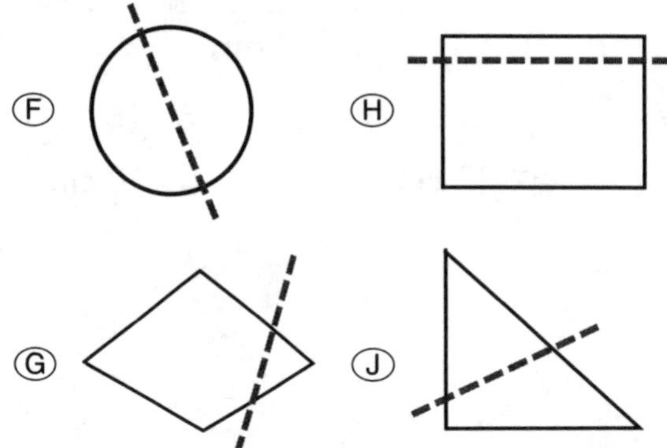

7 **Which figure has no parallel sides?**

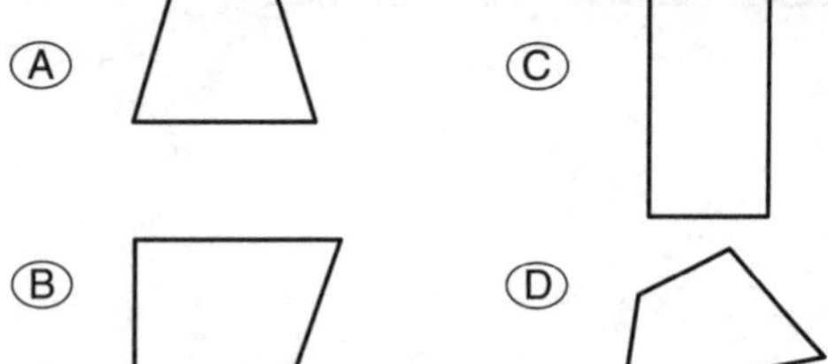

8 **Look at the map. Oak Street runs parallel to which street?**

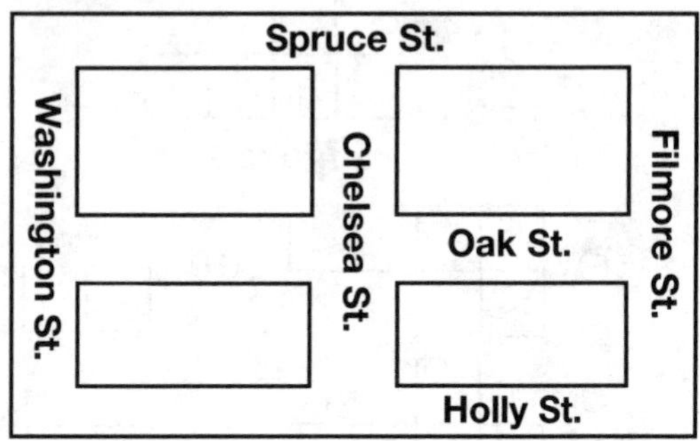

Ⓕ Holly Street　　Ⓗ Chelsea Street
Ⓖ Filmore Street　　Ⓙ Washington Street

9 **Which pair of lines will not intersect?**

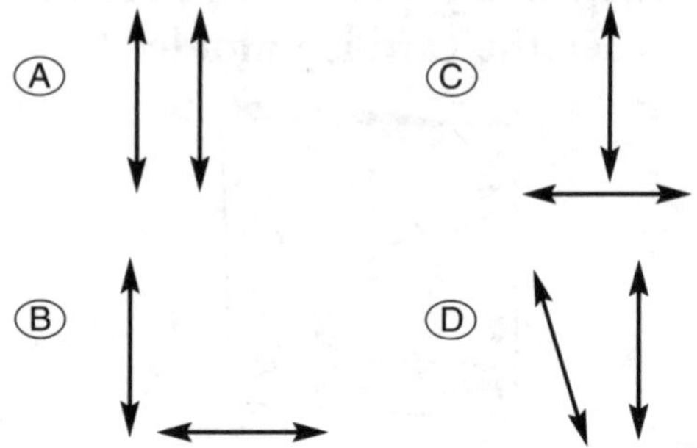

10 **What is the perimeter of this figure?**

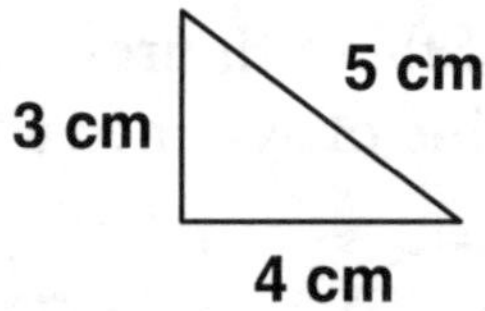

Ⓕ 6 cm　　Ⓗ 35 cm
Ⓖ 12 cm　　Ⓙ 60 cm

11 **Mrs. Eli hung a rope on all four sides of her new sidewalk to keep people off until the concrete dried. The sidewalk is a rectangle 3 yards long and 1 yard wide. How much rope did Mrs. Eli need to use?**

Ⓐ 3 yards　　Ⓒ 6 yards
Ⓑ 4 yards　　Ⓓ 8 yards

12 **Which figure has the largest area?**

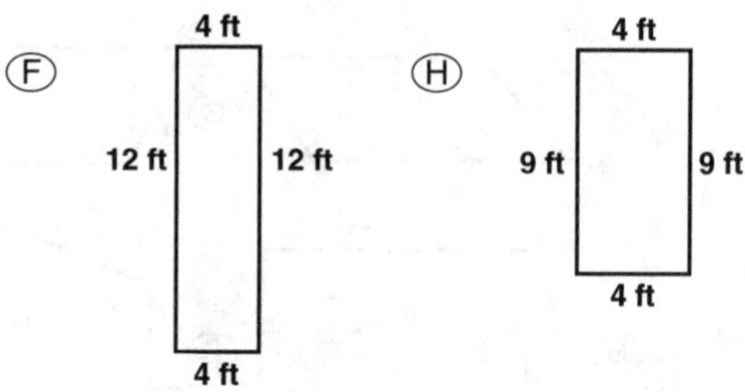

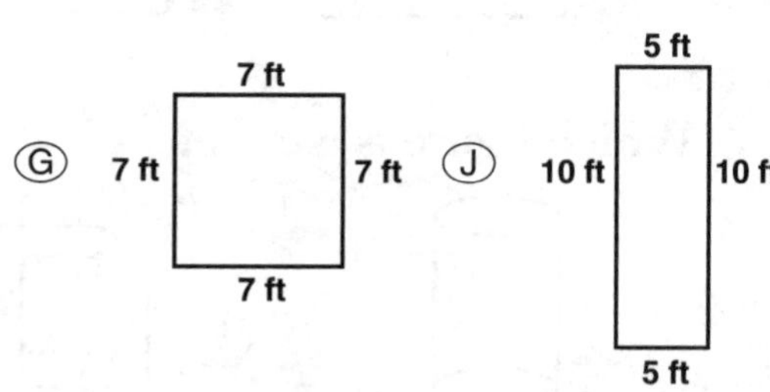

13 **The city pool is 10 meters wide and 20 meters long. What is the area of the pool?**

Ⓐ 10 m^2　　Ⓒ 200 m^2
Ⓑ 30 m^2　　Ⓓ 2000 m^2

14 **Katie twirled this banner in a parade. Which of these could not be Katie's banner?**

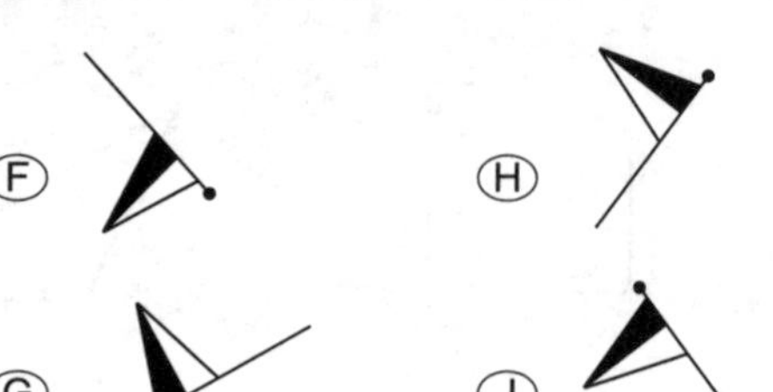

SCORE	14

MATH TEST

Directions
Choose the best answer to each question. If your answer is not given, mark "None of these."

The families in Mark's neighborhood are planting a community garden. Answer numbers 1–4.

1 **Mark opened a box with 24 packages of carrot seeds in it. He gave 8 packages to Kim. How many packages did he have left?**
Ⓐ 14
Ⓑ 16
Ⓒ 18
Ⓓ 22
Ⓔ None of these

2 **Last weekend the Porter family planted 15 new tomato plants in the garden. The Yamato family planted 37 new tomato plants. What was the total number of new tomato plants the two families planted?**
Ⓕ 22
Ⓖ 42
Ⓗ 48
Ⓙ 52
Ⓚ None of these

3 **Kim wants to plant 20 pea plants in 4 equal rows. How many plants will be in each row?**
Ⓐ 3
Ⓑ 4
Ⓒ 5
Ⓓ 6
Ⓔ None of these

4 **There are 8 summer squash plants in the garden. Each plant has 4 squashes growing on it. How many squashes are there in all?**
Ⓕ 12
Ⓖ 24
Ⓗ 28
Ⓙ 36
Ⓚ None of these

Ty and Pam are running the fishing game booth at the school carnival. Answer numbers 5–9.

5 **It costs 2 tickets to play the fishing game. Enrico played the game 12 times. How many tickets did he use on the fishing game?**

Ⓐ 14
Ⓑ 24
Ⓒ 26
Ⓓ 36
Ⓔ None of these

6 **A player can trade in 3 small prizes for 1 big prize. Marisa and Shawna have 15 small prizes to trade in. Which number sentence should you use to figure out how many big prizes they can get?**

Ⓕ $15 \div 3 = \square$
Ⓖ $15 + 3 = \square$
Ⓗ $15 \times 3 = \square$
Ⓙ $15 - 3 = \square$
Ⓚ None of these

7 **Ty and Pam had 455 large prizes when they opened the fishing booth. They have 247 left. How many large prizes have they given away so far?**

Ⓐ 202
Ⓑ 208
Ⓒ 212
Ⓓ 218
Ⓔ None of these

8 **This morning 122 people played the fishing game. This afternoon 189 people have played the game so far. Which is the best estimate of how many people have played the fishing game so far today?**

Ⓕ 200
Ⓖ 250
Ⓗ 300
Ⓙ 350

9 **On Friday, 992 people came to the carnival. On Saturday, 1311 people came. Which is the best estimate for the total number of people who came to the carnival?**

Ⓐ 1900
Ⓑ 2000
Ⓒ 2100
Ⓓ 2300

Students are selling wrapping paper and other gift items for school. Answer numbers 10–14.

10 **Mrs. Garcia ordered one roll of wrapping paper for $4.50 and one bag of bows for $2.35. What was the total cost of her order?**

Ⓕ $6.55 Ⓗ $7.05

Ⓖ $6.85 Ⓙ $7.45

11 **Tara's order totaled $8 for two of these items. Which two items did she buy?**

Ⓐ cards and wrapping paper

Ⓑ wrapping paper and ribbon

Ⓒ a candle and ribbon

Ⓓ ribbon and cards

$5.75

12 CARDS

$4.50

$3.50

$2.25

12 **One student was making a fruitcake for the bake sale. He put $\frac{1}{8}$ cup of raisins and $\frac{3}{8}$ cup of apple bits in a bowl. How much fruit was in the bowl all together?**

Ⓕ $\frac{4}{16}$ cup Ⓗ $\frac{1}{2}$ cup

Ⓖ $\frac{5}{8}$ cup Ⓙ $\frac{1}{4}$ cup

13 **Maria bought $\frac{1}{3}$ pound of walnuts, $\frac{1}{3}$ pound of pecans, and $\frac{2}{3}$ pound of almonds. How many pounds of nuts did she buy in all?**

Ⓐ $\frac{3}{4}$ lb Ⓒ $1\frac{2}{3}$ lb

Ⓑ $1\frac{1}{3}$ lb Ⓓ $1\frac{3}{4}$ lb

14 **One roll of shiny silver paper is 12.5 feet long. How long would 3 rolls be?**

Ⓕ 36 ft Ⓗ 37 ft

Ⓖ 36.5 ft Ⓙ 37.5 ft

15 **Hal is looking for his friend Jake's apartment. The apartment number is two hundred forty-five. Which of these is the number?**

Ⓐ 24.5 Ⓒ 254

Ⓑ 245 Ⓓ 2405

16 **Some students arranged chairs in the auditorium for the fourth graders' play. They put 20 chairs in the front row, 22 chairs in the second row, and 24 chairs in the third row. If they follow the same pattern, how many chairs will they put in the fourth row?**

Ⓕ 25 Ⓗ 28

Ⓖ 26 Ⓙ 32

17 **Nell is in line at the movie theater. There are exactly 9 people in line ahead of her. What is Nell's place in line?**

Ⓐ first Ⓒ ninth

Ⓑ eighth Ⓓ tenth

18 **What is 5436 rounded to the nearest ten?**

Ⓕ 5000 Ⓗ 5440
Ⓖ 5400 Ⓙ 5430

19 **Which is another way to write two and six tenths?**

Ⓐ 2610 Ⓒ 2.06
Ⓑ 260 Ⓓ 2.6

20 **What number tells how many blocks are in the picture?**

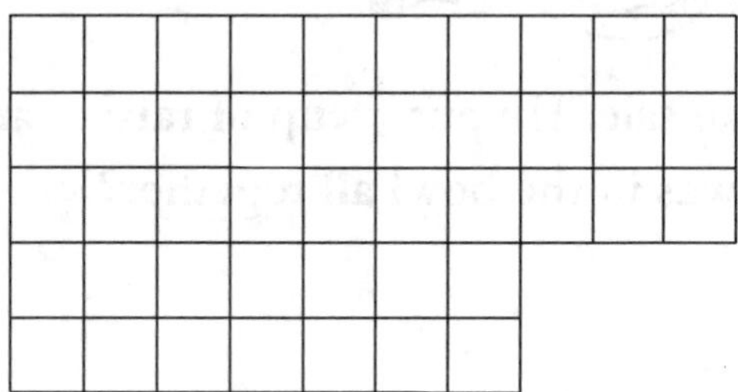

Ⓕ 40 Ⓗ 46
Ⓖ 44 Ⓙ 56

21 **Ben has four U.S. coins in his pocket. Which of these amounts of money could he have?**

Ⓐ 64 cents Ⓒ 83 cents
Ⓑ 76 cents Ⓓ 92 cents

22 **Which of these makes the number sentence true?**

$\frac{1}{4} > \square$

Ⓕ $\frac{1}{3}$ Ⓗ $\frac{1}{5}$
Ⓖ $\frac{1}{2}$ Ⓙ 1

23 **Fran's house number is an even number. Which of these could be Fran's address?**

Ⓐ 3611 Rose Street
Ⓑ 405 Elm Drive
Ⓒ 2889 Jackson Road
Ⓓ 110 Beach Court

24 **Jim is estimating the number of trading cards he and his brother Tom have. Jim has 102 trading cards. Tom has 87 trading cards. If Jim estimates to the nearest ten, which numbers should he use?**

Ⓕ 100 and 90
Ⓖ 100 and 80
Ⓗ 105 and 85
Ⓙ 110 and 90

25 **The pictures show the number of trading cards Jim, Tom, and their friends have. Which of these shows the trading card collections arranged from the most cards to the fewest cards.**

Jim 102

Tom 87

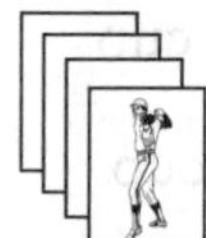
Rita 112

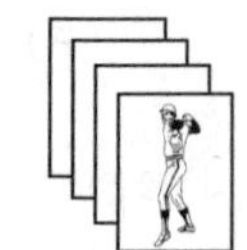
Sal 89

Ⓐ Rita, Jim, Sal, Tom
Ⓑ Tom, Sal, Jim, Rita
Ⓒ Jim, Tom, Rita, Sal
Ⓓ Rita, Sal, Tom, Jim

26 **Which of these shows how you should write the number on the sign in words?**

Ⓕ eight hundred thirty-six and four tenths
Ⓖ eight thousand three hundred forty-six
Ⓗ eight thousand three hundred sixty-four
Ⓙ eighty-three thousand six hundred forty

Directions

Peter kept track of how many birds he saw during a class field trip to a nature park. Then he made a graph of the results. Use the graph to answer questions 27–30.

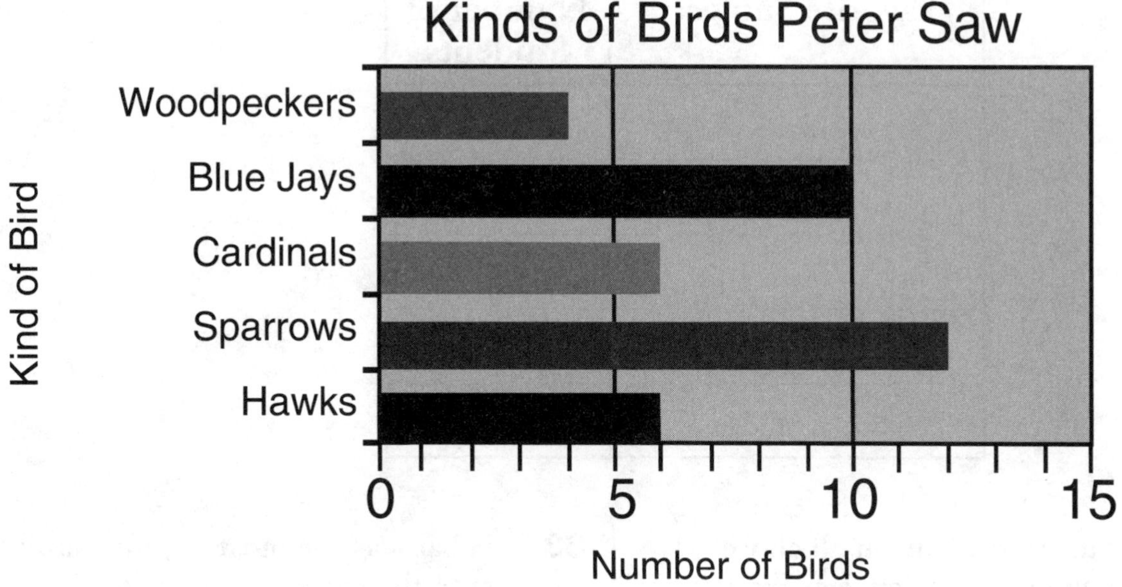

27 **According to Peter's graph, what kind of bird did he see the most of?**

Ⓐ blue jay
Ⓑ cardinal
Ⓒ sparrow
Ⓓ hawk

28 **How many more hawks than woodpeckers did Peter see?**

Ⓕ 2
Ⓖ 4
Ⓗ 5
Ⓙ 8

29 **Peter's friend Kendra saw 5 cardinals. How many cardinals did Peter and Kendra see all together?**

Ⓐ 10
Ⓑ 11
Ⓒ 13
Ⓓ 15

30 **Peter saw the same number of which two kinds of birds?**

Ⓕ hawks and cardinals
Ⓖ blue jays and sparrows
Ⓗ cardinals and sparrows
Ⓙ woodpeckers and blue jays

Directions

This table shows the school subjects students in Mr. Lee's class chose as their favorites. Each student chose one favorite subject. Use the table to answer questions 31–34.

Favorite Subjects	Number of Students
Art	5
Language Arts	5
Math	4
Science	3
Social Studies	6

31 **How many students in all chose social studies or science as their favorite subjects?**

Ⓐ 3
Ⓑ 6
Ⓒ 9
Ⓓ 18

32 **How many more students chose math than science?**

Ⓕ 1
Ⓖ 2
Ⓗ 3
Ⓙ 4

33 **What was the most popular subject with the students who voted?**

Ⓐ Language Arts
Ⓑ Math
Ⓒ Art
Ⓓ Social Studies

34 **There were 5 students absent the day the class voted. When they came back to class, 2 of them voted for Math, 2 for Language Arts, and 1 for Science. After these new votes are added, which two subjects will have the same number of votes?**

Ⓕ Art and Language Arts
Ⓖ Language Arts and Math
Ⓗ Math and Social Studies
Ⓙ Social Studies and Science

35 **Use an inch ruler to answer this question. How long is the fish?**

Ⓐ 1.5 inches
Ⓑ 2 inches
Ⓒ 3 inches
Ⓓ 7 inches

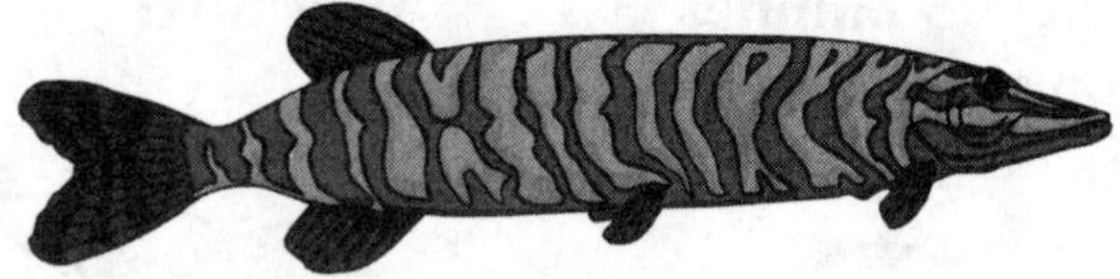

36 **The clock shows the time that Emma arrived at Lily's house. If it took her 12 minutes to get from her house to Lily's house, what time did Emma leave home?**

Ⓕ 3:18
Ⓖ 3:22
Ⓗ 3:24
Ⓙ 3:42

3:30

37 **Gail picked strawberries for 1 hour. Which is the most likely amount she picked?**

Ⓐ 4 cups
Ⓑ 40 gallons
Ⓒ 4 quarts
Ⓓ 40 pounds

38 **Thermometer A shows the temperature at 6:00 A.M. Thermometer B shows the temperature at noon. How did the temperature change during that time?**

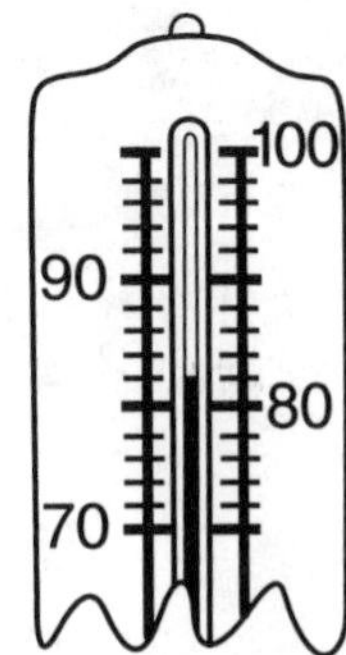

Thermometer A

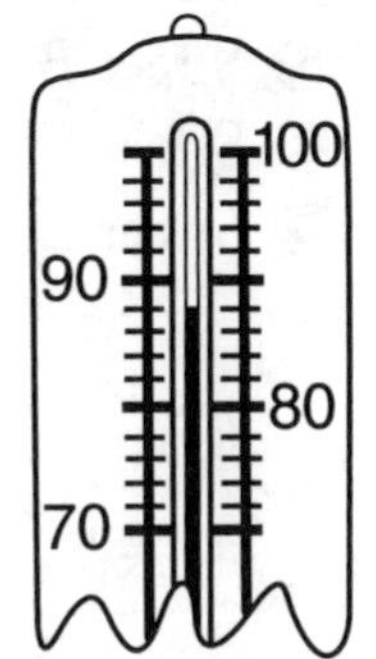

Thermometer B

Ⓕ It got 3 degrees warmer.
Ⓖ It got 3 degrees cooler.
Ⓗ It got 6 degrees warmer.
Ⓙ It got 6 degrees cooler.

39 **Bailey's birthday is exactly one week before Alex's. Alex's birthday is marked on the calendar. What day is Bailey's birthday?**

JULY

						1
Alex's 2 birthday	3	4	5	6	7	8
9	10	11	12	13	14	15
16	17	18	19	20	21	22
23	24	25	26	27	28	29
30	31					

Ⓐ June 24
Ⓑ June 25
Ⓒ July 8
Ⓓ July 9

40 **Use a centimeter ruler to answer this question. Which object measures 3 centimeters longer than the match does?**

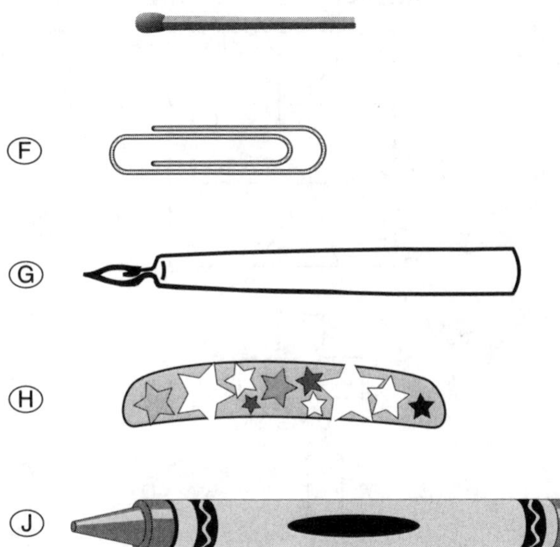

41 **Taylor's swim practice starts at 4:45 P.M. Taylor got to practice 15 minutes early. Which clock shows the time Taylor arrived at practice?**

Ⓐ 

Ⓒ 

Ⓑ 

Ⓓ 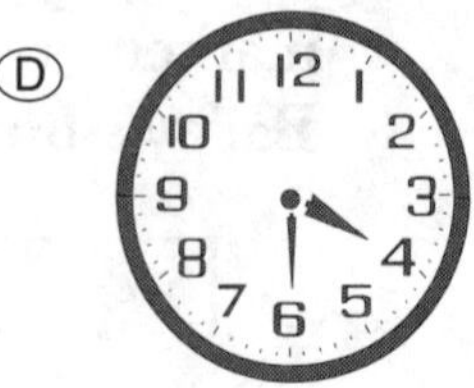

42 **Sharise folded each of these shapes in half. Then she opened them back up. In which shape did the two halves look the same?**

Ⓕ 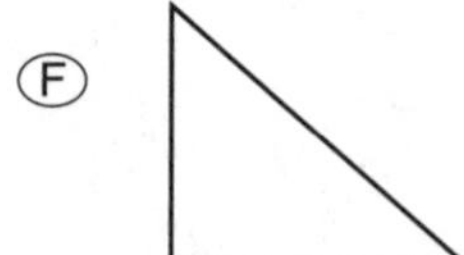

Ⓗ 

Ⓖ 

Ⓙ 

43 **Which of these pieces would complete the puzzle?**

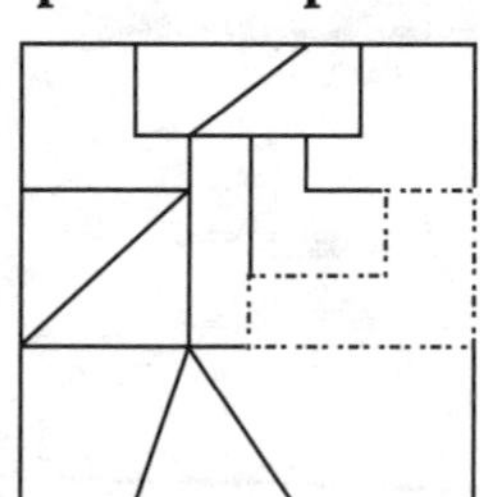

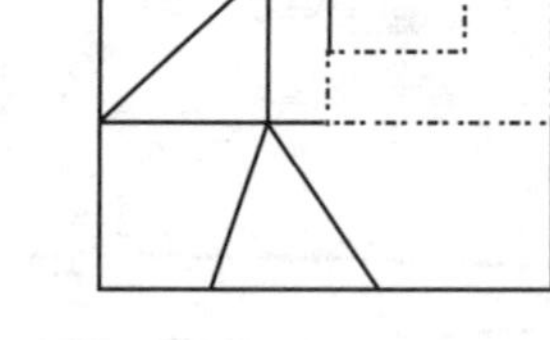

Ⓐ 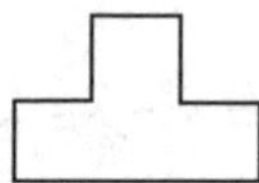

Ⓒ 

Ⓑ 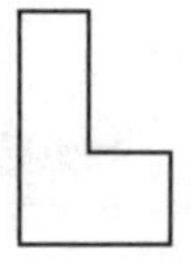

Ⓓ 

44 **How many *more* blocks would fill this box?**

Ⓕ 2
Ⓖ 4
Ⓗ 6
Ⓙ 8

45 **Port Street is perpendicular to Harbor Street. Which of the streets in the picture could be Port Street?**

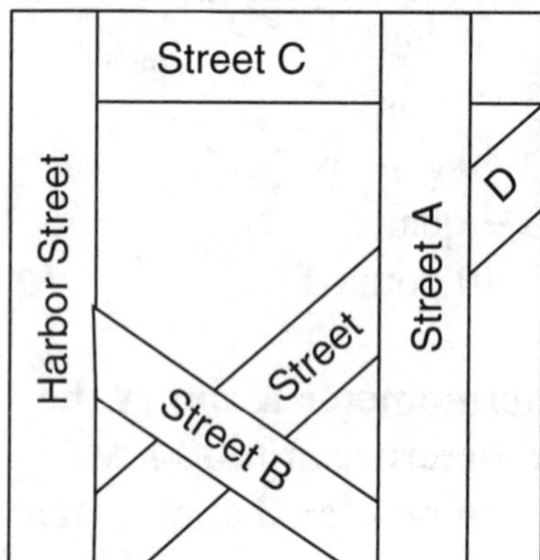

Ⓐ Street A
Ⓑ Street B
Ⓒ Street C
Ⓓ Street D

46 **Mr. Blaine wants to put a fence around his vegetable garden. How much fencing will he need to go all the way around the garden?**

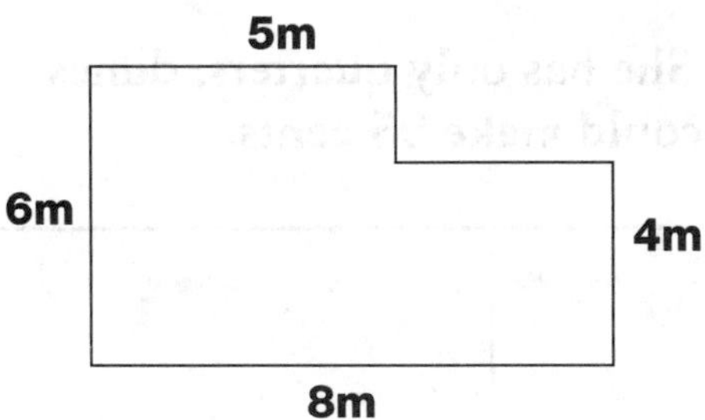

Ⓕ 14 m
Ⓖ 24 m
Ⓗ 28 m
Ⓙ 48 m

47 **Which of these shows a flip of Figure X?**

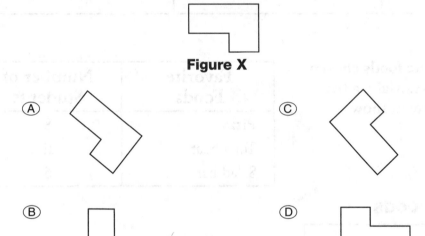

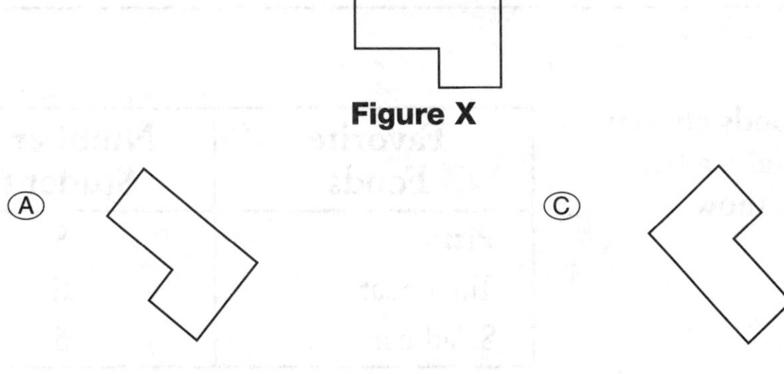

48 **The picture below shows the area of the playground. Which of the other pictures has the same area as the playground?**

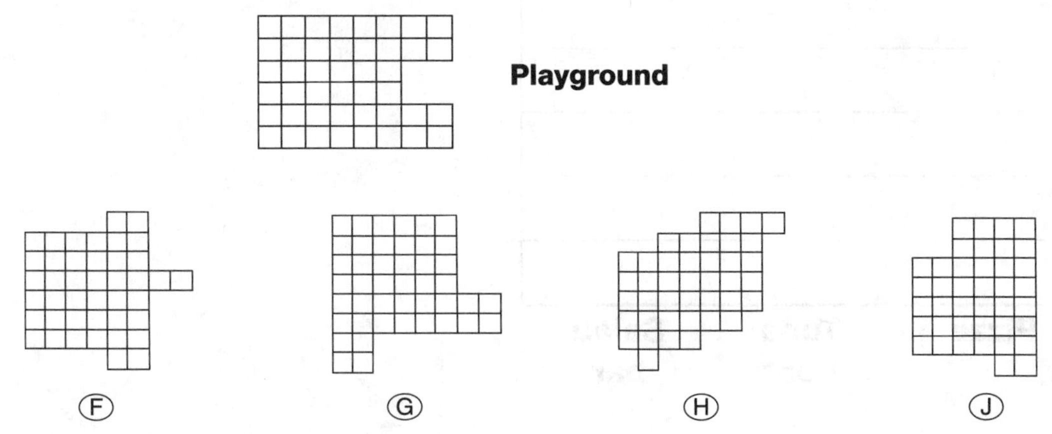

Directions
For questions 49 and 50, write and/or draw your answers in the spaces provided.

49 **Bonnie needs 95 cents to pay for a comic book. She has only quarters, dimes, and nickels. Show three different ways that she could make 95 cents.**

50 **The chart shows favorite foods chosen by students in one class. Make a bar graph on the grid below to show this information.**

Favorite Foods	Number of Students
Pizza	8
Tuna boat	11
Salad bar	6

Favorite Foods

Pizza	Tuna boat	Salad bar

Directions

To answer numbers 51–70, compute. If your answer is not given, mark "None of these."

51

$$\begin{array}{r} 76 \\ +\ 22 \\ \hline \end{array}$$

Ⓐ 54
Ⓑ 84
Ⓒ 88
Ⓓ 98
Ⓔ None of these

52

$$\begin{array}{r} 45 \\ -\ 36 \\ \hline \end{array}$$

Ⓕ 9
Ⓖ 11
Ⓗ 13
Ⓙ 19
Ⓚ None of these

53

$$\begin{array}{r} 112 \\ \times\ 2 \\ \hline \end{array}$$

Ⓐ 114
Ⓑ 124
Ⓒ 204
Ⓓ 214
Ⓔ None of these

54

$$\begin{array}{r} 115 \\ 321 \\ +\ 676 \\ \hline \end{array}$$

Ⓕ 1001
Ⓖ 1011
Ⓗ 1111
Ⓙ 1112
Ⓚ None of these

55

$$\begin{array}{r} 5.89 \\ +\ 3.00 \\ \hline \end{array}$$

Ⓐ 2.89
Ⓑ 5.92
Ⓒ 6.19
Ⓓ 8.89
Ⓔ None of these

56

$$\begin{array}{r} 6.7 \\ -\ 0.4 \\ \hline \end{array}$$

Ⓕ 7.1
Ⓖ 10.7
Ⓗ 6.11
Ⓙ 6.3
Ⓚ None of these

57

$176 - 39 =$

Ⓐ 133
Ⓑ 137
Ⓒ 145
Ⓓ 215
Ⓔ None of these

58

$$\begin{array}{r} 33 \\ \times\ 2 \\ \hline \end{array}$$

Ⓕ 66
Ⓖ 56
Ⓗ 55
Ⓙ 35
Ⓚ None of these

59

$\frac{1}{6} + \frac{5}{6} =$

Ⓐ $\frac{1}{2}$
Ⓑ $\frac{4}{6}$
Ⓒ $\frac{5}{12}$
Ⓓ $\frac{6}{12}$
Ⓔ None of these

60

$9\overline{)108}$

Ⓕ 9
Ⓖ 11
Ⓗ 12
Ⓙ 14
Ⓚ None of these

61

$325 \div 3 =$

Ⓐ 105
Ⓑ 107R2
Ⓒ 108R1
Ⓓ 109
Ⓔ None of these

62

$4 \times 3 \times 2 =$

Ⓕ 9
Ⓖ 10
Ⓗ 11
Ⓙ 14
Ⓚ None of these

63

$$\begin{array}{r} 345 \\ \times\ 5 \\ \hline \end{array}$$

Ⓐ 1505
Ⓑ 1525
Ⓒ 1705
Ⓓ 1725
Ⓔ None of these

64

$$\begin{array}{r} 8.1 \\ -\ 7.9 \\ \hline \end{array}$$

Ⓕ 0.8
Ⓖ 1.2
Ⓗ 0.2
Ⓙ 1.6
Ⓚ None of these

65

$$\begin{array}{r} 21\frac{2}{9} \\ -\ 6\frac{2}{9} \\ \hline \end{array}$$

Ⓐ 15
Ⓑ $15\frac{2}{9}$
Ⓒ 16
Ⓓ $27\frac{4}{9}$
Ⓔ None of these

66

$$\begin{array}{r} 35.5 \\ 6.2 \\ +\ 17.05 \\ \hline \end{array}$$

Ⓕ 59.2
Ⓖ 114.55
Ⓗ 58.75
Ⓙ 212.2
Ⓚ None of these

67

$1 - \frac{7}{8} =$

Ⓐ $\frac{1}{8}$
Ⓑ $1\frac{7}{8}$
Ⓒ $\frac{1}{7}$
Ⓓ $1\frac{1}{8}$
Ⓔ None of these

68

$11\overline{)133}$

Ⓕ 12 R3
Ⓖ 13
Ⓗ 13 R1
Ⓙ 13 R3
Ⓚ None of these

69

$6 \times 70 =$

Ⓐ 130
Ⓑ 420
Ⓒ 480
Ⓓ 4200
Ⓔ None of these

70

$30\overline{)900}$

Ⓕ 0.3
Ⓖ 3
Ⓗ 30
Ⓙ 300
Ⓚ None of these

SCORE	/70

Answer Keys

Problem-Solving Strategies
PRACTICE 1: TEST

1. C
2. G
3. D
4. F
5. D
6. H
7. A
8. F
9. 450 − 52 + 85 = 483 stamps
10. 96 ÷ 8 = 12 CDs

Using Whole Numbers
PRACTICE 2: TEST

1. D
2. F
3. D
4. H
5. A
6. J
7. D
8. K
9. C
10. F
11. 15 × 5 = 75 people
12. 13 + 4 + 8 = 25 birds
13. A
14. F
15. B
16. K
17. D
18. H
19. A
20. J

Using Fractions and Decimals
PRACTICE 3: TEST

1. C
2. J
3. D
4. F
5. B
6. K
7. 3.75 miles
8. 2/5 of the bar is left.
9. C
10. J
11. A
12. K
13. B
14. H
15. D
16. G

Number Concepts
PRACTICE 4: TEST

1. A
2. H
3. A
4. G
5. A
6. J
7. B
8. H
9. D
10. G
11. D
12. F
13. C
14. H

Interpreting Data
PRACTICE 5: TEST

1. A
2. H
3. D
4. F
5. B
6. G
7. C
8. F
9. D
10. G
11. [Vertical bar indicating 100.]
12. 100

Measurement
PRACTICE 6: TEST

1. B
2. J
3. B
4. H
5. D
6. G
7. C
8. J
9. C
10. G
11. C
12. 50 kilometers

Answer Keys, continued

Geometry
PRACTICE 7: TEST

1. B
2. H
3. B
4. J
5. A
6. F
7. D
8. F
9. A
10. G
11. D
12. J
13. C
14. F

Math Test

1. B
2. J
3. C
4. K
5. B
6. F
7. B
8. H
9. D
10. G
11. D
12. H
13. B
14. J
15. B
16. G
17. D
18. H
19. D
20. G
21. B
22. H
23. D
24. F
25. A
26. H
27. C
28. F
29. B
30. F
31. C
32. F
33. D
34. H
35. C
36. F
37. C
38. H
39. B
40. G
41. D
42. J
43. B
44. H
45. C
46. H
47. D
48. G
49. Accept all combinations that equal 95 cents. Examples of possible answers: 3 quarters and 2 dimes; 2 quarters, 4 dimes, and 1 nickel; 1 quarter and 7 dimes.
50. The graph should show vertical bars for Pizza (8), Tuna boat (11), and Salad bar (6).
51. D
52. F
53. E
54. J
55. D
56. J
57. B
58. F
59. E
60. H
61. C
62. K
63. D
64. H
65. A
66. H
67. A
68. K
69. B
70. H